Association
of America

# Communicating with Your Staff

Karla Powell

*Skills for*

*Increasing*

*Cohesion and*

*Teamwork*

# Communicating with Your Staff
*Skills for Increasing Cohesion and Teamwork*

Additional copies of this book may be ordered by calling 800 621-8335.
Mention product number OP208799

ISBN 1-57947-000-9

BP37:0157-00:12/00

# Contents

## Introduction

Who greets your patients and recognizes if they seem harried, irritated, worried, or upset? Beginning with your front desk and throughout your practice, your staff gathers information about your patients that, as their physician, you should know. Conversely, your patients hear and see things about your staff that could hurt or help your practice. A cooperative patient may witness a difficult staff encounter, making that patient wonder about the quality and direction of her care.

Physicians typically seek the tangible and quantifiable. The fluidity of communication, though, resists containment. Much like the human body, communication is mutable, potentially irksome, somewhat mysterious, and yet fascinating. If physicians can attune their ears to subtle sounds within the heart's chambers that reveal its condition, is that effort really so different from training one's ear and instincts to decipher what one's own staff reveals?

To prosper in a modern medical practice, you may have to refine your notions of effective communication. Consider for a moment just who is the all-important link between your patients and you. Your staff is that link. Whatever their positions, all staff members serve as an extension of an organization's goals and values. The authoritarian model of communicating limited *instructions* may hamper staff's ability to fulfill the goal at hand, which is good patient care. New communication strategies are about expanding possibilities by communicating useful *information* that empowers your staff.

To survive in the current economic climate, businesses recognize that communication can no longer operate strictly from the top down. Today, communication must filter up, down, and across the organizational chart. Smart leaders realize that barriers to communication disrupt, rather than enhance, their staff's efforts, both individually and as a group.

### Setting the Stage for Effective Communication

This book explores new methods of business communication that can enhance your practice. These techniques have been adapted to the needs of medical practices, as the practice of medicine is distinct from other ventures.

The first of the three chapters in Part I focuses on a communication model. Even though communication is part of daily life, it is a good idea to take a few moments to consider just what communication sets out to accomplish. The communication model in Chapter 1 is highly practical, taking into account how good communication flows and how miscommunication crops up. Chapter 2 centers on how to better offer and accept criticism, resolve conflict, and build cohesion among your staff. These two chapters are complemented by Chapter 3 on cultural competence. The diversity of today's medical staffs means that cultural assumptions and styles should be factored in when thinking about how to enhance communication in a medical practice.

By recognizing and respecting the variety found among human beings, you can work with the likenesses—and work around the differences. Differences in style, in emphasis, and in outlook will always exist. How differences are handled often determines whether your practice will be the best it can be. To set the tone of leadership, conflict and criticism must be turned from negatives into positives. (This important issue is discussed in Chapter 2.)

## Refining Communications Techniques

The second part of this book focuses on techniques of communication. Chapter 4 describes different management styles, how to assess which style is yours, and ways of adapting your style to make communication flow more freely in the office.

Chapters 5 and 6 center on two fundamental management techniques: empowerment and collaboration. By empowering your staff, you will make them more autonomous and more effective. By maximizing collaboration among individuals, teams, and departments, you will raise the quality of patient care offered by your practice group. Both empowerment and collaboration require constant attention to effective communication techniques. As your staff is empowered and works collaboratively, communication becomes central in meeting their goals and raising the organization to new levels of success. Good communication fuels staff achievement, which is fostered through greater communication.

Chapter 7 is a close look at one of the major themes of the book: the harmonious team. Cooperation is crucial in the modern organization, which is less hierarchical than in the past. Teamwork is required to get the work done and to enhance patient satisfaction. Communication is the major ingredient in creating harmony and cooperation in a medical practice. Chapter 8 examines a specific aspect of communication: How can physicians and staff members make the best use of burgeoning technology? There is more equipment available than there ever has been, and the capabilities of much of this machinery are extraordinary. This chapter gives tips on how to blend technological wizardry most effectively into a medical practice.

Finally, Part II ends with a chapter on morale. Keeping staff members' morale high relies almost exclusively on the quality, timing, and channels of communication in an office—in short, its communication culture. A staff with high morale can meet almost any challenge gracefully and efficiently. Without a major effort at understanding communication and communicating well, though, physicians cannot lead their staff members to improve patient care—the central purpose of a medical practice.

Good communication creates strong bonds between physicians and staff members—in fact, among all of the people who work collegially in your medical practice. Your staff is your vital link to your patients. Value and openly appreciate them for the good they contribute to your practice. What is good for your staff is good for your practice and good for your patients.

# Part I

# Understanding the Basics of Good Communication

Ziqin asked Zigong: "When the Master arrives in another country, he always becomes informed about its politics. Does he ask for such information, or is it given him?"

Zigong replied: "The Master obtains it by being cordial, kind, courteous, temperate, and deferential. The Master has a way of enquiring which is quite different from other people's, is it not?"

Excerpted from *The Analects of Confucius,* translated by Simon Leys (New York, NY: W. W. Norton; 1997).

# Chapter 1

# Understanding the Communication Process

Consider this: American executives spend 94% of their time communicating. Good communication skills have long been seen as an asset in the business world for their value in negotiation, persuasion, and motivation. Business people use their skills to communicate outside of their organizations—with vendors, lawyers, competitors, and clients—as well as within the organization with staff members and colleagues.

## Good Communication for Organizational Health

If you assume communication requires no effort on your part, you may find yourself contending with unforeseen complications of a different sort. In today's medical practice, it does not suffice just to communicate well with your patients. You must also communicate well with your staff members, as they are the vital link in the delivery of high-quality health care between you and your patients.

Your relationship with your staff is entirely different from your relationships with your patients. Your staff is not looking to you for your medical acumen; staff members are looking to you for leadership. And like any good leader, you must first recognize opportunities and differences—and then you must respect differences in personality and style among those you are expected to lead. You must also make use of these differences to the best advantage so that you and your staff can achieve your common goals.

## How Do We Communicate? A Model

In their book, *Communicating at Work*, Tony Alessandra, PhD, and Phil Hunsaker, PhD, offer a model for how we communicate. According to Alessandra and Hunsaker, communication involves the following five components:

A speaker → encoding → a message → decoded → by a recipient

Let's consider each of these components. Let's also begin to consider what factors or behaviors can help or hinder communication.

1. ***Speaker.*** The speaker is the person who wishes to send a message. The speaker also encodes the message. To encode a message, speakers rely on their backgrounds, education, sense of style, good manners, and training, which may differ from their audience.

2. ***Encoding.*** Encoding the message involves word choice, gestures, and tone (tone of voice in an oral communication and tone of the language in a written communication). As we encode the message, we face the possibility of making mistakes. What if we choose a word that the recipient is unlikely to know the meaning of? What if the word is ambiguous and likely to be misunderstood? Do our gestures and facial expressions conflict with the sense of the message? What is the appropriate tone? Almost everyone distinguishes tone quite easily and can tell if the speaker is too loud, too soft, unassertive, threatening, too literary, too informal, or uninterested.

   For example, encoding applies in the common situation of whose turn it is to take out the garbage:

   *"Out!" [while pointing to the offending bag of trash].*

   The information may be conveyed, but the gesture may be encoded inappropriately—and there could also be a tone problem.

   *"Please take out the immondizie."*

   Unless you live in a household that is bilingual in Italian and English, your choice of words may simply flummox the listener.

   *"You always try to avoid responsibility, and here's a perfect example: all this garbage that I'd like you to take out right now."*

   The vocabulary is clear, but the tone may be a problem. Further, this sentence contains more than one message.

3. ***Message.*** The message is of great importance. In this book, you will find a great deal of information and advice about tone, consensus, and flow of communication. These factors all affect how a message will be received, but you should not neglect the message itself. In the previous example, at least three messages are conveyed: You're irresponsible. You've gone and done it again. Take out the trash. Should your audience receive so many messages at one time? What is the appropriate message for this meeting, staff retreat, performance review, or holiday card? Should certain information be saved for another time and place? What order of presentation should the information follow?

4. ***Decoding.*** During decoding, your listeners take your words and translate them into terms they understand. Because each person brings differences in background, education, and attitudes to each communication, each person will decode your message

uniquely. While decoding is not fraught with hazards for you or your message, it is an area where misunderstanding can develop.

In her book, *Multicultural Manners: New Rules of Etiquette for a Changing Society*, Norine Dresser describes how yellow flowers are decoded in two cultures. Anahid, an Armenian woman, brings yellow flowers to Mrs Golestani, whose daughter is away on her honeymoon. In Armenian culture, yellow flowers mean "I miss you." Mrs Golestani, who is Iranian, becomes visibly angry.

What message did Mrs Golestani receive from the yellow flowers? In Iranian culture, yellow flowers are a symbol of hatred. Each woman brought her past experiences, customs, and etiquette to the situation, but the message that Anahid had encoded as "I miss your daughter" was decoded by Mrs Golestani to mean "I am an enemy." (Chapter 3 will explore such issues in more detail.)

5. **Recipient.** As shown in the anecdote about giving yellow flowers as a gift, recipients bring their training, education, sense of self, etiquette, and personal history to a message. To deliver a message effectively, speakers must encode it in such a way that their listeners have little trouble in decoding it properly. How to present complicated messages to your staff members effectively is a central theme of this book. When dealing with colleagues who are highly trained and share a common purpose, you may find that your common medical language and familiarity with medical practice will make decoding by the recipients easier. (When you discuss management issues, though, you may not be able to make the same assumption.)

Another issue is distraction, which can disrupt the simple model of communication that we are working with. Confucius, who was concerned with proper communication throughout his career, once said, "What was unique in Yan Hui was his capacity for attention whenever one spoke to him" (*The Analects of Confucius*. W.W. Norton, 1997). Yan Hui evidently was not easily distracted, but he also seems to have been an active listener. (Techniques of active listening will be discussed later in this chapter.)

## Four Temperaments, Four Styles

Dozens of complex and involved theories of human nature abound. They often stem from early philosophers' and physicians' theories about the makeup of the body and about how to treat wounds and disease. Hippocrates, by far the most influential of these early physicians, incorporated the four humors: blood, phlegm, yellow bile, and black bile (which he believed were the main bodily fluids), into his diagnoses. Each bodily fluid was thought to promote certain kinds of behavior, and an imbalance in the fluids, leading to excesses of one of them, was believed to be the cause of disease.

However, as Guido Majno points out in his book, *The Healing Hand: Man and Wound in the Ancient World*, this fourfold division was not new even in Hippocrates' time. Some Greek philosophers believed that the basic elements of the universe were air, fire, earth, and water, and we still think of the year as progressing through four seasons. These patterns of four were often related to each other so that, for example, each of the four humors was tied to a season of the year.

In the second century AD, the Greek physician Galen expanded the theory of the four humors. Because of Galen's great prestige well into the Renaissance, thinkers in all disciplines—from William Shakespeare to William Harvey—have expounded on the ancients' wisdom about temperament. We still use the terms from this theory to describe emotions and impulses: *melancholy* derives from black bile, and the adjectives *sanguine* (blood), *choleric* (yellow bile), and *phlegmatic* (phlegm) derive from the other humors. A character dominated by black bile was melancholic, whereas blood led to an exuberant personality. Yellow bile made a person irritable and aggressive, and phlegm made you lethargic.

In the 1920s, Carl Jung was among the first psychiatrists and physicians to classify personality types using the new psychological ideas then being explored and refined by a number of scientists, including Sigmund Freud. Jung presented his theory and classification of styles of behavior in his treatise, *Psychological Types*. In 1962, Isabel Myers and her mother Kathryn Briggs published *The Myers-Briggs Type Indicator*. Based on their ideas about Jung's theories and classification, the Myers-Briggs Type Indicator (MBTI) is a questionnaire widely used to analyze the attitudes and actions of four personality groups. More recently, the Myers-Briggs concept was adapted by David Keirsey into another assessment tool—the Keirsey Temperament Sorter—again using a fourfold classification.

As Guido Majno mentions, though, the word *temperament* comes from the Latin for *blend* or *mixing*. Few people will show personality traits only of one type—a fact that leads to human diversity as well as to the occasional miscommunication. The MBTI, in fact, recognizes 16 basic types based on the following four scales:

- Extraversion-Introversion
- Sensing-Intuition
- Thinking-Feeling
- Judging-Perceiving

Thinking in terms of scales (rather than four humors) enables you to assess your own attitudes and behaviors more subtly. This more detailed way of assessing personality types can be applied to styles of communication as well.

## Four Styles of Communicators and How They Interact

Theories about individual communication style also group behavior into four primary types, taking into account newer thinking about how people with various temperaments interact in the workplace. What follows is a brief overview of four major kinds of communicators.

### Directors

Directors are more interested in the task at hand than in the personalities involved. They are often goal-oriented and prefer a structured environment that meets their own agenda. They want to know the "how" of things, rather than the "why." Highly independent, they may view planning or supervision as merely means to their own ends. They work through people, rather than with them, and they often tap key people and key procedures for their usefulness toward achieving their own goals. The director may easily climb a hierarchical ladder to reach the top.

If your personality is dominated by the following characteristics, you are likely to be a director:

- Decisive and competitive
- Controlling and impatient, with a tendency toward involving yourself in conflict
- Autonomous and independent
- Fast-paced, task-oriented worker who likes to get things done
- Cool and distant demeanor
- Comfortable with change

### Relaters

Relaters are those who prize their relationships with others. Human relationships are their main source of satisfaction. Relaters may prefer a supporting role and leave the limelight to the dominant types. They are good facilitators and are often in the helping professions allied to physicians—such as nursing, social work, and psychology. If you are a fan of the television show, *ER*, think of Nurse Hathaway, who turned down the chance to get her MD once she realized that she would have to get on a track that hampered her caring role with patients. Relaters are typically more comfortable dealing with emotions than the more controlled types—the thinkers and directors—would be. If allowed, relaters can be an invaluable resource for a director during decision making, as directors sometimes lose sight of the person behind the patient.

As mentioned, the relater is the personality type most devoted to cultivating ties with others. If you find the following characteristics in yourself or another, you may have discovered a relater:

- Slow to act or decide and averse to risk
- Supportive and a good listener
- Lacking in self-direction, and has a strong need to belong
- Preference for working cohesively and a dislike of conflict
- Comfortable with closeness, and a good counselor
- Dislike interpersonal conflict

### Socializers

Socializers are your staff's "people" persons. They enjoy inclusive activities and do not like to work by themselves. They are familiar with their co-workers and work well with others. Typically, they are consensus-builders who dislike conflict and are more flexible with their time and duties than directors or even relaters, who also prefer to adhere to procedure. Perhaps you recognize some of the socializer qualities in your practice managers, who may be called upon to be all things to all people.

Like relaters, socializers are oriented mainly toward creating and maintaining relationships, eased by the qualities mentioned above and those following:

- Spontaneous and energetic
- Frenetic and enthusiastic
- Persuasive and imaginative
- Likely to seek validation and involvement
- Tendency to generalize and exaggerate

### Thinkers

Thinkers are more likely to be found in research, surgery, or other specialties that require methodical evaluation of risks and results—unlike directors, who may jockey for the position of medical director or other action-oriented endeavors. These specialties also give thinkers a chance to work by themselves and to avoid conflict, which they prefer. Thinkers identify closely with their work and less so with their relationships at work. They share some traits with relaters, such as being averse to conflict, collegial about sharing information, and not being as aggressive as directors. But unlike relaters or socializers, thinkers are not looking for conversation. Perhaps even more so than directors and relaters, thinkers do not do well with role ambiguity.

They do not shift gears easily, as do socializers. Focusing on their work is what makes them tick.

What matters to thinkers are careful evaluation, problem solving, and often a need to be right. If you find that you value the following qualities in yourself and others, you may fall into this category:

- Judicious and deliberate
- Detail-oriented and analytical
- Highly organized and structured
- Objective and rational
- Factual and precise

## Playing Against Type

Now that you may have discovered that you are a thinker in an office full of relaters, how should you act on your understanding of yourself and your surroundings? If you are a thinker, you may have to scale back your perfectionism and seek out involvement in the flow of communications and activities in the office. Relaters may have to leave the web of human relations that they so enjoy for other opportunities and challenges. Socializers may have to rely less on their usual reward: the approval of others. Both relaters and socializers, because they are people-oriented types, have a tendency to neglect negotiation skills and their problem-solving abilities. Directors may have to learn to give up control—always an important issue for them—and become more supportive.

In many cases, playing against type will involve developing your listening skills and looking for the nonverbal cues that come with communication. If you return to the basic model of communication offered previously in this chapter, you can see how each personality type will differ when it comes to decoding a message.

## What Goes Unsaid Is Part of Communication

The last quarter of the last century has yielded research suggesting that 65% of meaning stems from nonverbal behavior, with some claiming that nonverbal cues carry almost twice the weight of speech. Nonverbal cues vary from individual to individual, culture to culture, religion to religion, and man to woman.

The basic model for communication includes encoding—the point in the process when the speaker chooses words, gestures, facial expressions, and tone. Words serve as vessels to carry thoughts and feelings to another person's consciousness. But, as mentioned previously, the processes of encoding by the speaker and decoding by the recipient involve the deeper waters of personal attitudes, beliefs, values, experiences and biases.

Although it is clear that nonverbal behavior sends a strong message, it is not always clear whether the message conveyed is what was intended. Popular claims to the contrary, you cannot read another like a book through "body language." Physicians learn that a physical symptom can indicate any number of conditions, and the same can be said of nonverbal suggestions.

Does poor eye contact indicate a deception or shyness? To further complicate communication, in some cultures avoiding eye contact is a way of showing respect for authority. Does someone's tone of voice or demeanor indicate displeasure with what you have said, or is it that you caught the person at a bad time?

Likewise, yawns, giggles, whispering, or crossed legs and arms can easily be misinterpreted. Within the same culture, nonverbal communication is ambiguous and at best can only be inferred. Nevertheless, as hard as it may be to describe how we perceive nonverbal communication, we have all been trained through years of watching and interpreting our gestures and movements and those of other people we deal with. We can trust our instincts about some nonverbal displays, so do not dismiss your powers of observation.

Although we may generally understand how Americans communicate, cross-cultural reactions to how something is said still apply. Because American culture is so complicated, you may find that your style of communication and reactions differ from someone who was born in a different region of the United States or who grew up surrounded by a certain ethnic group or social class. Because we consider ourselves a nation of immigrants—a country built by continual waves of newcomers—you undoubtedly will be in contact with staff members and patients who were born outside of the United States and for whom English may not be their first language. When communicating with people from foreign cultures, it is best to learn their gestures and mannerisms before drawing any conclusions. (We will explore some of these differences in Chapter 3.)

## Listening Goes Against Human Nature

So much of what we learn throughout the educational system is about how to convey our own thoughts and ideas. We are taught precious little about how to receive another's thoughts and ideas. How do we deal with this complicated communication process involving words, gesture, and culture? By listening. Listening is hard work. Fortunately, we may be built for listening. A fragment from the writings of first-century philosopher, Epictetus is still a good model for communication among physicians, administrators, nurses, and technicians, whether male or female: "Nature hath given men one tongue but two ears, that we may hear from others twice as much as we speak."

On the other hand, in his book, *Effective Listening: Hearing What People Say and Making It Work for You*, Kevin Murphy comes across as more skeptical:

> Listening is the accurate perception of what is being communicated. It is the art of separating fact from statement, innuendo, and accusation.

> Listening is a process in perpetual motion. It begins when one hears or observes what is being said, continues as one stores and correlates the information, then begins again with one's reaction.

> Listening is not the simple ability to decode information; it is a two-way exchange in which both parties involved must always be receptive to the thoughts, ideas and emotions of the other. To be an effective listener, one must not only open the lines of communication and relax; one must compel others to do the same.

> What else is listening?

> Listening is a natural process that goes against human nature.

Saint Jerome, the fifth-century biblical scholar and translator, was even tougher on those who do not develop their listening skills: "No one cares to speak to an unwilling listener." When physicians order tests, it is to verify the "message" they received from the patient exam. It is a form of listening. Further, good leaders recognize that *every* member of their staff can convey critical information, if they simply lend a willing, well-trained ear. This skill has even been given a special name: *active listening.*

You may learn what procedures are hindering efficiency, what patients are griping about in the reception area, and what concerns are expressed over the phone. The gathering of facts and information through active listening gives power—power to reshape your organization, power to make decisions about procedures, and power to create a cohesive, pleasant work environment. Given the number of articles written lately about the Internet and the wonders of easily accessible data, you probably have heard many times that information is power.

Active, or skillful, listening offers many benefits. It has the capability to improve morale, as it will show your interest in your staff. You will discover how your staff perceives their own jobs and what motivates them. By listening actively, you can learn what your staff members consider to be appropriate rewards and an appropriate management style. You may even discover, by listening well, that a person who seems to be having trouble at work may in fact be in the wrong job (or in a poorly defined job). Active listening also offers you the opportunity to clarify misconceptions and involve all staff in the overall process of running your practice.

Active listening may be seen as a way of verifying the message received during conversation. The techniques of active listening involve eliminating distractions, repeating important points, and ensuring that speaker and recipient agree on what message is being conveyed. Further, to ensure that the speaker's message is conveyed accurately, the listener must ask questions and offer feedback.

## Eliminating Interference

Ineffective listening is linked to organizational problems that range from low morale to lost profits. (More on morale in Chapter 9.) Time constraints and other competition for our attention are major culprits to ineffective listening, as are personal biases. These barriers to receiving messages include assumptions about what is going to be said (which tune out what actually *is* said), preconceived ideas about the speaker or topic based on one's own values and beliefs, lack of empathy, emotional reactions to the speaker's appearance or manner of speech, and other distractions that interfere with the message itself.

What follows is a step-by-step process to help you better hear what is being said. Applying these techniques will help make you a more active listener, help you better able to focus on what the person with whom you are conversing is telling you, and make you less likely to be distracted by outside factors.

**Step 1: Pay attention.** Eliminate or minimize extraneous distractions, such as noisy passersby, ringing telephones, or unnecessary visitors. If a certain level of distraction is unavoidable, make an effort to concentrate so that you stay focused. Two ways of focusing on the conversation include rephrasing what has been said and maintaining eye contact. When you are listening to others, pretend you are back in school. Imagine having a pop quiz on what they are telling you.

**Step 2: Encourage your speaker through positive reinforcement.** Notice how often you offer reinforcement to the speaker during a telephone conversation with simple responses like "yes," "okay," and "hmm." These simple cues can keep a telephone conversation going. During face-to-face conversation, you can encourage the speaker to continue by smiling or nodding your head. Normally, we also add vocal prompts such as "go on" or "I see" to keep the information flowing. Be careful to display attentive body language to indicate to the speaker that they are not being tuned out. Crossing one's arms or looking away are two ways guaranteed to end a conversation—they both signal impatience. Also, some people find it intimidating to discuss matters over a large desk. If office furniture seems to impair the flow of conversation, find a simple table and chairs in a quiet space instead.

**Step 3: Keep the conversation flowing.** Communication is a two-way street. Gridlock occurs when a speaker becomes frustrated by lack of response. Have you ever been to a job interview where the interviewers expect you to do all the talking, while they sit in stony silence taking cryptic notes about what you say? Does that make you feel tense and even slightly suspicious? By responding to what the speaker says, you encourage the speaker to *refine, expand,* or *correct* the message. If you are silent, the speaker may simply repeat the message. It is better for you to test what you are hearing. Rephrasing statements helps to create agreement, too. In fact, careful rephrasing is a good technique to adopt because repeating points in different words enables both the speaker and recipient to clarify the message:

A: *I'm having trouble getting to work on time.*

B: *Are you having trouble getting to the office on time in the morning? Can you tell me why you are having trouble getting to work on time?*

A: *I just seem to have trouble getting here in the mornings. I'm taking that evening course, so maybe I'm just too tired.*

B: *Since you are taking the evening course, your normal schedule seems to be thrown off. Would it help if you changed your flextime schedule so that you started a half-hour later?*

A: *I've always worked the same schedule here, but I'm beginning to think that I would like a change.*

**Step 4: Rein in your emotions.** Listen to the whole message, and avoid reacting to minor issues. If you're having a negative emotional reaction to your speaker, think of what you may have in common, rather than your differences. Remember, when that speaker is a member of your own staff, the most important idea you share is the desire for a pleasant and productive practice that delivers quality patient care. Check your value judgments when you are listening to another.

Don't block the meaning of his or her words because of superficialities such as speech patterns, idiosyncrasies, appearance, or image. (Rephrase instead to avoid getting "stuck" on an idiosyncrasy.) It is also important to keep in mind that the speaker is usually looking to you to solve a problem, and no matter how emotionally the matter may be presented to you, mixing in your own feelings will not solve the issue.

## Speaking and Listening Effectively to Enhance Your Work

When communication works, work is made easier. Physicians are called upon to make daily judgment calls that those in the business world can only imagine. No physician takes this responsibility lightly. Painstaking effort is made to eliminate any margin for medical error, and communication mistakes, which are often just as costly, should be a focus of your efforts as well.

This chapter presented a model for communication that showed a simple process of getting a message from the speaker to the recipient. The process, however, is not perfect, and subsequent chapters consider differences in style, potential for conflict, and cultural factors in communication.

### Bibliography

Alessandra T, PhD; Hunsaker P, PhD. *Communicating at Work.* New York, NY: Simon & Schuster; 1993.

Confucius. *The Analects of Confucius.* Translated by Simon Leys. New York, NY: W.W. Norton; 1997.

Dresser N. *Multicultural Manners: New Rules of Etiquette for a Changing Society.* New York, NY: John Wiley & Sons; 1995.

Jung C. *Psychological Types.* Princeton, NJ: Princeton University Press; 1976.

Keirsey D. *Please Understand Me II: Temperament, Character, Intelligence.* Del Mar, CA: Prometheus Nemesis Book Co.; 1998.

Majno G, MD. *The Healing Hand: Man and Wound in the Ancient World.* Cambridge, MA: Harvard University Press; 1975.

Murphy K. *Effective Listening: Hearing What People Say and Making It Work for You.* New York, NY: Bantam Books; 1987.

Qubein N. *How to Be a Great Communicator: In Person, on Paper, and on the Podium.* New York, NY: John Wiley & Sons; 1996.

## Web Sites of Interest

For more information on David Keirsey's work on temperaments, see www.keirsey.com.

For details on the Myers-Briggs Type Indicator and many related forms and publications, see Consulting Psychologists Press at www.cpp-db.com/products/mbti/index.html.

# Chapter 2

# The Three C's: Offering Criticism, Resolving Conflict, and Building Staff Cohesion

Any hint of conflict conjures up negative images. When conflict is at its worst, we experience it as a stressful drain of our energy. At a minimum, we think of conflict as a colossal time-waster. Many of us would admit that our idea of a perfect world is a world free of conflict. But you may as well wish for a world free of illness as for a world free of conflict.

In our complicated modern society, we receive criticism every day. Try not to think of *criticism* as a synonym for a barrage of negative comments—and the breeding ground for serious conflicts. Instead, think of criticism in its broader definition as an assessment of behavior or performance usually given verbally or on paper. If the criticism that we receive is thoughtful, we will actually value it.

This chapter begins by examining how to deliver helpful criticism. A properly considered assessment of another person's performance generally will not become a source of conflict. In fact, by helping others to make course corrections (and by showing that you take their opinions and concerns seriously), you will be building staff cohesion within your medical practice.

## Criticism: Make It Constructive

How many times have you read a review of a movie or a book (written by a person who claims to be a critic) and wondered whether you had seen the same film or read the same biography as the critic? Critics often stumble by letting their personal agendas come through in their review. A critic who believes that only impressionist painting is worthy of the name of art will make an unfair assessment of other schools of painting. Yet painters who explore other styles besides impressionism have much to show the viewer. Similarly, you may have encountered people in the office who believe that there is only one way to do things and who will not allow others to deviate. They only take the impressionist school seriously.

Another pitfall of critics is failing to deal with a work on its own terms. A critic may resist what a movie is trying to relate—and dismiss the film and the actors' performances as "unbelievable."

In the first case, the critic has made it clear what he plans to communicate, while the critic in the second case is telling us what information she allows herself to receive. In the first instance, the critic's preconceived agenda limits communication with others. In the second, the critic is unwilling to receive a communication being offered. In both cases, the critics have focused exclusively on their own feelings and perceptions. What the other person is trying to say becomes secondary. Whether the critic has considered and assimilated the information being offered by the other person—who may be a director, painter, receptionist, or anesthesiologist—is not as important as shoring up the critic's own perceptions.

Criticism cannot be avoided. One of the characteristics of modern society is that most of us live in urban areas, where we have constant contact with other people. Further, many people now work for complex organizations such as schools, hotels, restaurants, law offices, computer consultants, police departments, and medical practices. In medical care, there is a strong trend away from the sole practitioner. Even the self-employed and family farmers work with clients, buyers, vendors, and insurance companies.

Working in large organizations means that one's performance will be evaluated. Delivering an assessment of a staff member's performance can clear the air, lead to a rethinking of each person's positions, and afford an opportunity to exchange valuable information about attitudes toward work, all of which are important. You may even find that the recipient does not agree with your criticism.

## Criticize Well to Avoid Defensive Reactions

Still, there are ways to handle criticism that will maintain working relations and could improve them. Whether you are the one delivering criticism or on its receiving end, there is always the potential for a pattern of defensiveness by the speaker and the recipient that can lead to misunderstandings. Following are three general ideas to keep in mind so that you can make criticism an objective assessment rather than bitter medicine that we all have to take to hold a job:

1. ***What actually needs to be corrected?*** Focus on behavior. No one goes to the office to hear (or have it implied) that he or she is a disgrace or a bad person. By focusing on behavior, you alert people to matters that they can change.

   Avoid discussions of personality:

   > *"The reason you are late so much is that you have a short attention span."*

   Focus on changing the behavior instead:

   > *"I am worried about your being late from time to time. How can we resolve this? Is it a matter of how your work hours are scheduled?"*

2. ***How exactly should the other person change?*** Deal with the other person's issues more than your own issues. The reason that you are offering criticism is so that the other person can assimilate it and put it into action. You may have to settle for a compromise based on the other person's capabilities and comfort with change. Save your broader agenda for a staff memo, where you can set forth general ideas and standards.

   Avoid blanket statements that may seem self-serving:

   > *"In this office, we are never short with patients. It is not acceptable."*

   Instead, your criticism should promote change:

   > *"I'm not sure that you handled that conversation with Mrs Burlington as well as you could have. In the future I'd like you to focus more on listening to patients, even if they repeat information."*

3. ***Is this the appropriate timing for this issue?*** Focus on the present and on the situation at hand. It is best to have a short memory about past slights and mistakes. If the problem is of long standing, you will not resolve it in one session (and you may have to explain why it was never noticed).

   It is not effective to bring up old news:

   > *"You filed this information incorrectly, so I went into the files and discovered that everything is misfiled all the way back to 1996."*

   Begin the resolution of the problem by focusing on current behavior:

   > *"I wanted to speak to you about something that you did last Tuesday. I'd like to clarify our filing procedures."*

Besides the general rules that criticism should be focused, offer suggestions that can be accomplished. Following are some specific tips for preparing for a talk with a staff member:

- ***Do not criticize anyone in front of other people.*** Many organizations take pride in their freewheeling staff meetings and their informal atmosphere. Blurting out your perceptions of someone's shortcomings is likely to bring a pause to the general discussion—any noise you hear may be the sound of your reputation in free fall. It almost goes without saying that you should not criticize someone in front of the people she supervises. While it happens, it is inadvisable. If you must discuss an issue with a staff member, find a quiet place, preferably an office with a door that shuts.

- ***Focus on one issue at a time.*** In the description of the model of communication in Chapter 1, some of the perils of encoding and decoding were highlighted. It is best in a potentially tense situation to give one message at a time—and to ascertain that the recipient understands the message. Work through your concerns in succession. Don't deliver a litany of complaints. Focus on one or two issues in a single meeting. If there are more issues, save them for other meetings.

- *Get your facts straight.* Criticism relies on objectivity. If you tend toward the director or thinker personality type described in Chapter 1, you are likely to be more comfortable working simply with the facts of a situation. If you are a relater or a socializer, you will have to check your tendency to rely on relationships. Most people appreciate objectivity, so do your research. Bring in documentation if necessary (but do not threaten people with documents as if you were in a courtroom).

- *Stick to those facts.* Be prepared to provide specifics so that the other person gets a clear picture of the less-than-optimal behavior. Names, dates, and dollar amounts may be needed (and call for more research). Sticking to the facts, though, gives shape to the discussion, as you should go through the facts in an orderly way to give clear examples of behavior that is not working out. Further, by showing specifically what has not been effective behavior, you give the person an opportunity to visualize how to change habits and procedures to make things work smoothly. How can someone know what to do if the criticism you offer is a vague "We need to collect our receivables faster"?

- *Offer an incentive for change.* If a positive response to the criticism could result in an improved situation for the person being criticized, make this apparent. If you would like to make the change into a job goal that will be measured and assessed when it comes time for performance reviews and raises, say so. Vague exhortations to improve rarely produce results in the workplace. While most people take pride in their work, they also want to be measured against an objective and quantifiable scale.

## Frame a Positive Delivery

You should emphasize areas of respect and appreciation while offering suggestions for improvement. One of the reasons for having your discussion in an office with the door shut, for example, is to show your respect for the other person's position and accomplishments. Although you may not be able to eliminate the negatives entirely, they do go down easier when you also frame your message positively. After all, you already have a working relationship with the other person, which you want to continue.

Acknowledge any way that you may have added to the problem. Even if it is a minor point, such a concession sometimes takes the sting out of criticism. Follow that up with a willingness to help create a solution.

## Consider the Source

Sometimes it is not enough to gauge what is said and how it is said. Sometimes it is as much a matter of *who* says it. We are all more willing to take suggestions about our behavior from those for whom we feel rapport, respect, or admiration. Criticism is more likely to be received well if you build on a rapport that has already been created and if you rely on the practice's structure to designate the proper source.

Among professionals, peers may be the proper source. In a group medical practice, you work with a number of physicians as colleagues and equals. Sometimes, a situation will require that you offer criticism to a professional colleague. You may find giving criticism of your peers to be awkward, but you should rely on your common training and common professionalism, which build a strong rapport, to help those involved to focus on the facts and the behaviors in need of change. You are unlikely to find a third party with the qualifications to offer criticism to your fellow physicians.

Concern for respect and rapport, however, does not mean that supervisors can avoid dealing with their own direct reports. The structure of a practice—who is assigned to train and supervise another staff member—normally is organized so that there is a proper source of criticism. If you lean toward the relater or socializer personality type, you may have a tendency to rely on the person's web of relations to help fix a situation. This tactic is not likely to work. "Dr Papandreou thinks that you leave the office too early on Fridays" may sound like a simple message for a peer to deliver. The nurse being criticized will wonder why Dr Papandreou cannot speak for herself and why his attendance has been discussed with one of his officemates.

Keep in mind that no matter how justified the criticism, whoever delivers criticism must have some bearing on the situation and the authority to offer the criticism. Supervisors are in charge of their subordinates and serve as the channel of criticism from other members of the practice. If the problem has overwhelmed the person's supervisor, someone higher up in the organization may be called in to mediate and deliver criticism. The person's supervisor should still be at the conference to show that all affected parties are aware of the situation.

People who tend toward the director personality type are often much too eager to offer criticism. If you are a director type, make a point of remembering that the criticism must come from the proper source. If you are not the proper source, you must defer to the person who is. Learn to work with staff supervisors, your practice administrator, internal committees, and the personnel department if necessary. Otherwise, your colleagues may think of your freely offered critiques as static to be tuned out or, worse, challenges that can only be settled through conflict.

Some organizations like to have their personnel departments step in, especially if a serious matter of job performance is at issue. The hope is that the representatives from personnel can serve as objective listeners and mediators. Some managers find, however, that the people in human resources do not frame issues clearly, largely because they are not familiar with the details of every employee's procedures. This lack of familiarity makes it hard to describe exactly how the staff member should change to resolve the issue. Often, after meeting with the "objective" third party, the employee returns to the department feeling put out because he does not understand why he is being criticized—and somewhat angry at finding out that someone broke departmental solidarity to "tell tales out of school." In short, if your problem really is "local politics," keep criticism within the department where it belongs. Otherwise, criticism will invariably become a source of conflict.

## On the Receiving End

Offering criticism can be a wrenching experience, and learning to do it well takes some creativity. Each of us also has to learn how to receive criticism. If the criticism is justified and delivered well, we can discuss the matter with our critic and come to some resolution. Often, justified criticism is not delivered well. The person who is criticizing you may harbor no ill will, knows that the situation is easily corrected, and may even have a possible solution, but the message can get garbled on its way to you. If the message was not encoded well, how can you decode it to settle the situation to everyone's satisfaction?

If you sidestep criticism, you will only cause the situation to fester. Parrying criticism does not make the problem go away. In any case, there are ways to absorb criticism without either striking back or avoiding a resolution.

By seeking detailed explanations, you and your critic focus on what specifically has caused the problem and, by extension, how both of you can sketch out a solution together. This response is not limited but instead fosters further communication. You come to a face-saving middle ground, not allowing denial yet also not donning a mantle of guilt and blame. This middle ground is where you negotiate. (Keep in mind that relaters and socializers especially need to work on their negotiating skills.)

To reach this middle ground, you can try several tactics to clarify your critic's message:

- ***Ask for details if the criticism seems unclear or unfounded.*** This is especially important if your critic is a relater or a socializer, as these types tend to focus on relationships rather than facts. They tend to offer too few details, as they may not want to seem petty and overbearing. On the other hand, thinkers will have lists of details, and you may have to help sort them out so that you both understand which details have priority. Directors tend to move quickly—and often without a lot of detail, which they consider boring. If you can understand the director's general thrust, you may want to begin negotiations. If not, ask for details, and extract them gently.

- *Seek examples of why your behavior is inappropriate.* If your critic is a relater or socializer, their criticisms may be framed to highlight human relationships—you have slighted someone, you are affecting the cordial office atmosphere, you do not take enough time to cultivate the other members of the staff. Directors and thinkers tend to focus on tasks, so their criticisms may center on missed deadlines, reports with misspellings, lateness to meetings, differences of opinion about prescriptions or tests, or slips in procedure. You may have to translate the examples to fit your style. For example, you may be affecting the cordial office atmosphere (a relater criticism) because you expect to submit reports with misspellings (a director shortcoming). On the other hand, you may find that your tendency to rely on your own judgment about prescriptions and tests (a thinker tendency) is perceived as a lack of collegiality (a flaw from the point of view of socializers).

- *Offer your own assessment of what the trouble is.* This is an opportunity for you to make sure once more that your style of communication meshes with the message and style of the critic. If you are a thinker, for example, you tend to work methodically, autonomously, and carefully. Your first concern would be to offer details. If your critic is a socializer (a fast-paced "people person" with less regard for facts), your list of details may come across as boring and irrelevant, possibly even as an evasion.

- *Reiterate how you hear the complaint about yourself being expressed.* It is important to describe the matter so that your critic believes that you understand what is troublesome about your behavior. You may have to rephrase or refine your description in light of that person's communication style. A relater may want to explore your feelings and motivations, while a director may want a quick admission of fault and a plan of action. You may not want to discuss personal matters with a relater, and you may find the director's approach way too brash. Do not focus on what may bother you about their styles of communication. Negotiate instead. (After all, you do not have to give away the store.)

Once you have clarified the issue causing trouble, it is time to settle on a resolution to the matter. Ask for solutions or other feedback that provides more insight into the complaint. Keep styles of communication in mind. You have to understand the solution offered by your critic. You should make sure that a resolution is reached that each of you can live with. "I just write little notes of apology whenever something likes this happens," proposes the relater, causing consternation in a director or a thinker, neither of whom meant to offend. In this case, a thinker would have to explain to the relater making the criticism that the proposed solution would not work. "Little notes of apology sound like froth and potential lawsuits to me," is not the best answer from a thinker, however, even if that is how they do appear to her.

The relater has just indicated that he relies on such gestures and thinks them important. Instead, the thinker should come up with a mutually satisfactory way to mend frayed working relationships or procedures.

## Defuse the Situation

Sometimes, you may feel that conflict is building and that it would be better for all involved to calm the situation quickly. One tactic is beautiful in its simplicity—and usually works. Swiftly agreeing with another person's criticism of you can stop him in his tracks.

You likely will not even lose face by adopting this approach. You can limit yourself to agreeing with the facts, "Yes, I admit I've been tardy lately." Then you can go on to point out mitigating circumstances or how this lapse contrasts with your otherwise exemplary work performance. Often, the critic is greatly relieved, as what she fears most is having to tell something uncomplimentary about you that you may not have noticed, thus implying that you are both inept at work and lacking in self-awareness. She may have foreseen a long exchange and an unhappy response from you when you realized that behavior that you considered normal has come up for criticism. Once you agree to the facts, though, it is best not to wrangle about a solution.

A second widely used tactic for defusing criticism has less likelihood of success. You may agree with someone's right to respond when offering criticism, even if he or she is unfairly blaming you for the situation. For example, if you promised to hire part-time clerical support for your practice manager only to learn that a hiring freeze has been announced, you may need to hear out his or her frustrations. You may in fact have done nothing wrong, for example, if human resources gave you mistaken information. You still can acknowledge your practice manager's right to complain. On the other hand, if you did indeed hear rumors about a hiring freeze and made a promise to your practice manager without verifying the rumor, you are at fault and should accept criticism.

## Understanding How Conflicts Arise

The many styles of communication can lead to misunderstandings. It is a fact of life that people with different standpoints do not always get along well. Further, modern medical care requires constant judging, assessing, and critiquing of practices and people. Minor conflicts over viewpoints and opinions arise often, and major conflicts are likely to happen with some regularity.

According to *Communicating at Work* by Alessandra and Hunsaker, "People naturally disagree about what to do and how and when to do it. That interaction of ideas and opinions sparks new ideas and leads to better solutions and plans of action. However, when differences of opinion are accompanied by too much emotional commitment to one point versus another, the resulting conflict can be damaging."

Managing conflict can be done with some of the skills and talents physicians use to manage illness. Many of the techniques for understanding criticism and negotiating solutions can be used to handle minor conflicts. Just as the worst advice you could give a patient about an ailment is "Ignore it and it will go away," such is the case with conflict.

## Conflict's Four Phases

Communications theorist Louis Pondy identifies four phases of conflict:

1. Latent

2. Perceived

3. Felt

4. Manifest

The first phase is the *latent* phase, akin to an early diagnosis. Conflict is often created whenever change occurs, particularly when two or more parties must now cooperate to achieve a desired objective. What industry has seen more change in recent times than health care? Further, this sweeping change has called for more teamwork, a movement away from the traditional top-down medical model. Because people are under pressure to change work habits and longstanding work relationships, the potential for misunderstandings, stress, and misgivings arises.

If things are left to fester, conflict worsens. As the conflict passes from the latent phase into the next phases, it becomes increasingly hard to resolve. The conflict becomes like a medical condition that is left untreated. Most conditions require some intervention to alleviate the symptoms.

The second phase of conflict is *perceived* conflict. Tensions mount because of a growing awareness that there is a problem, although those involved many not be sure where the root of that problem lies. The early, and continuing, repercussions of managed care resonated with free-floating anxiety and ambiguity. This is the stage when you might notice a lot of whispering around the proverbial water cooler.

The third phase of conflict is *felt* conflict. In this phase, the parties involved zero in on their differences, which intensifies perceived conflict. Frustrations gravitate toward specific issues, and individuals commit more to their respective positions. People may feel that they are forced to choose sides.

The final phase of conflict is *manifest* conflict. In this phase, individuals act out their differences through outward displays intended to frustrate one another. The conflict is full-blown at this point, which is the point when office politics take over everyone's lives, work begins to slow down, and the fighting is almost constant. Often, staff members will resign rather than stay in an unhappy, conflict-ridden organization.

To pursue the medical metaphor, early diagnosis is necessary to treat conflict. Once conflict reaches the manifest stage, resolution is that much harder. If conflict is acknowledged early on, co-workers may not become so attached to individual positions that any concession they make seems like defeat.

You can prevent staff conflicts from becoming a systemic disorder in your medical practice. The resulting staff loyalty and cohesiveness that arise from overcoming conflicts in your practice *together* as a group is the positive side of conflict. Just as ignoring conflict worsens problems, handling conflict well brings people closer.

## Conflict Under Control

Depending on what best suits the situation and personalities involved, a number of approaches for managing conflict are effective. With so many options, there is no good reason not to make an attempt to control conflict before it overwhelms you and your practice.

Of the four personality types, only the director is comfortable with conflict, in part because directors are at ease with change. Socializers, while they also enjoy change and variety, steer clear of conflict because of their relationship orientation. The other two personality styles are even less interested in conflict. Relaters value peace, enjoy the social aspects of work, and avoid risk, while thinkers prefer to work by themselves and do not care to be "dragged into" such tense situations.

Avoidance is the first approach that is sometimes mentioned when conflict rears its disorderly head. Often, someone in a meeting will suggest, "Well, let's just leave it alone for a while and see what happens." As an approach to conflict resolution, avoidance is fraught with uncertainty, requires a deft hand, and relies on careful observation. Avoidance is generally the least effective way of handling any situation involving more than one person. (You can be sure that two people in a continuing conflict have already decided to avoid each other.)

Avoidance may only work when you are sure that not reinforcing the behavior will cause the behavior to go away. A good example of avoidance (or *nonreinforcement*) is the employee who is late two days in row. Do you mention the lateness and risk a confrontation? Do you wait and see? The paradox is that mentioning the employee's lateness may in fact reinforce the staff member's behavior. In many instances, staff members will correct their own behavior without your intervention. Reinforcement may not be necessary.

Most of us vaguely hope that we can rely on avoidance so that we can skirt conflict and confrontation. Unfortunately, people and situations by and large do not right themselves through nonreinforcement. Instead, the situation continues to grow worse—through perceived conflict, choice of sides, hardened positions, and outright discord.

The following approaches to conflict resolution require action. They are more likely to produce results than avoidance.

1. **Accommodation, the Patched-Up Resolution.** Accommodation is only a temporary resolution. Accommodation makes it seem as if the parties to the confliction have agreed to cooperate, but it is really only a bandage on the underlying conflict. If one party gives in only because of pressure to paper over the conflict and does not have the opportunity to air his or her opinions, conflict remains latent. Additional stress may cause the smoldering conflict to jump into the next phases. Nevertheless, there are benefits to accommodation in that good relations may be renewed, something that may help in a situation in which the parties have had a breakdown in cordial, effective communication. However, accommodation is almost always dogged by suspicion that one of the parties has had to forfeit the privilege of freely airing his or her opinions—a feeling that can grow burdensome as the one who conceded continues to feel exploited by the cause of conflict and the resulting concession.

2. **Imposition, the Power Play.** Imposing the solution is the approach in which a superior decides to pull rank and force a resolution. A power play may work when everyone accepts the power relationship. Few managers have the wisdom and power of Solomon, however. A manager risks losing her reputation with all parties involved if the solution imposed does not seem appropriate or feasible to everyone. Obviously, imposition takes less time, as no negotiation is needed. Among the many drawbacks to this managerial style is that imposition can foster resentment if subordinates' needs are not met. Like accommodation, it also may fail to get to the root of the problem.

3. **Collaboration, an Attempt to Rebuild.** Collaboration is the flip side of the competitive, and rather authoritarian, approach of imposition. Collaboration requires both

cooperation by all parties involved and assertiveness by the person mediating the dispute. Collaboration takes a more creative approach, as well as a longer view, toward problem solving. The goal is not only to resolve the conflict, but also to improve relations. However, collaboration takes more time, and it may prove to be a bumpy ride toward a resolution if certain parties remain antagonistic.

4. **Compromise, the Way to the Middle Ground.** Compromise takes the middle ground to reach a solution that is agreeable to everyone. It is more often used when negotiating for tangibles, such as salary, workload, or hours. Although cooperation is involved, because each party concedes something to reach agreement, everyone is still acting in self-interest. By its very nature of give-and-take, compromise may not yield results deemed perfectly acceptable to all those involved in the conflict. Nevertheless, few people are truly uncompromising (unless your staff is made up only of pure director types). Most people understand that compromise will settle conflicts—and that compromise is always a bit rough around the edges.

## Cohesiveness: Bonding to Maximize Communication

When it is working well, the human body is a marvel of cohesiveness. If any of its separate elements break down, failure can undermine the health of the entire organism. It is much the same with the social organism that evolves when individuals work systematically toward a shared goal. If cohesion exists, the organization is vigorous, healthy, and adaptable. If cohesion is lacking, the organization's function is impaired, and it becomes sluggish, inflexible, and inefficient.

Certain conditions must exist in which to cultivate staff cohesiveness. These conditions can easily unravel if overlooked or neglected. Like human health, the health of organizations can be subtle and hard to monitor. Yet if you keep in mind the factors that contribute to cohesiveness and productivity, you can monitor these conditions and prevent any decay in the qualities that unify a work group.

Perhaps one of the most dramatic examples of optimal group effort is the construction of the Empire State Building in New York City. The Empire State Building went up during 1930 and 1931 at the rate of four-and-a-half stories a week. From architect to welder, widely disparate members of the group performed record-breaking feats in a united commitment to a mutual goal. Such things are possible with a unifying vision and sense of purpose.

Listed here are some ways to create better cohesion within a group:

1. ***Set shared goals.*** To attain or exceed shared goals, a group's momentum continues at a steady pace or even builds. Conversely, if group members do not share goals, cohesiveness suffers and individualistic behavior takes over. Although effective groups accept a certain degree of individualism, because individual enterprise also fosters new ideas, too much divergence from the shared goals and values of the group discourages cohesion.

2. ***Encourage reliance on the group.*** Security about where individuals stand within the group also contributes to cohesion. If that security is threatened, individuals become divisive and competitive until the cause of their anxiety is alleviated. Generally, their anxiety stems from having to make their own way within a tumultuous and dynamic group. When individuals rely on one another to get the job done, there is more unity than when group members work on discrete tasks removed from other group members.

3. ***Look for challenges.*** By encouraging competition with outside organizations or comparison against objective standards, you set challenges for the group. Group members can then focus their attention on the challenge rather than on the behaviors of other members of the group. External threats to a group invariably spur its members toward better cooperation—even if their typical way of doing business is normally somewhat improvised. You should remain leery of relying on external threats to build group cohesion, however. You may come off as Chicken Little announcing that the sky is falling and that only a concerted effort will save the organization. It is better to use outside organizations and standards as benchmarks and to customize your organization's response to their implied challenge.

## Managing Criticism, Conflict, and Cohesion

In this chapter, the three C's were discussed: criticism, conflict, and cohesion. Criticism and cohesion are central to building an effective, flexible, and productive organization. How criticism is given affects staff performance and morale. Criticism that is given well will raise staff standards and minimize staff turnover. Criticism and even conflicts are basic ingredients in staff cohesion, which rely on good staff morale, high standards, a common purpose, and free-flowing communication. Conflict is natural in organizations, especially in organizations undergoing great change or competing in dynamic industries. If you are concerned about criticism and staff cohesion, you may find that making an effort at handling conflicts among staff members actually becomes easier and is widely appreciated.

## Bibliography

Alessandra T, PhD; Hunsaker P, PhD. *Communicating at Work.* New York, NY: Simon & Schuster; 1993.

## Web Sites of Interest

To examine a range of articles and books, go to the Workplace Conflict Resource Center maintained by the Institute for Conflict Resolution (Bacal and Associates) at members.xoom.com/workconflict/index.htm.

Workplace Solutions is a consortium of professional mediators and crisis managers with a Web site at www.wps.org.

# Chapter 3

## Incorporating Cultural Diversity

In *Multicultural Manners: New Rules of Etiquette for a Changing Society*, Norine Dresser tells a story about red ink:

> Mrs Gussman is one of the best English teachers in the school. She spends every weekend reading her immigrant students' compositions and making careful comments in red ink. To soften her criticisms, she says something positive before writing suggestions for improvement, using the students' names to make the comments more personable. 'Jae Lee, these are fine ideas but….'
>
> These red-inked notes send shock waves through the families of her Korean students, but Mrs Gussman is unaware of this until the principal calls her into the office.

In American culture, red ink has slightly negative connotations. Teachers mark mistakes in red ink, as do proofreaders and editors. If your accountant starts to talk about red ink, you know that you are headed for financial trouble. How could writing notes in red ink prove to be shocking?

Koreans only write the name of a person in red ink at the time of the person's death or on the anniversary of a death. For that reason, the parents were highly upset to see their children's names written in red. In parts of Mexico and China, it is also offensive to write a person's name in red.

I think back to the communications model in Chapter 1. The Korean parents decoded a different message from the caring, cordial message that Mrs Gussman encoded. Often, conversations between people of different cultural backgrounds will founder because of customs, education, religious beliefs, and expectations that they may not share. Understanding other cultures helps in the encoding and decoding of messages.

Because the United States prides itself on being a nation of immigrants, most physicians will already have seen great variety of patients. Further, many physicians are immigrants, and they have learned to adapt to the communication styles and beliefs of native-born Americans.

In this chapter, the discussion focuses on cultural diversity—and cultural competence—in the office. The often-heard phrase, *culturally competent health care,* describes "a range of attributes, attitudes, behaviors, and policies that providers need to be effective in cross-cultural situations," according to Christine Hinz in *Communicating with Your Patients: Skills for Building Rapport*, a recent book from the American Medical Association.

## A Nation of Shifting Demographics

As Nido Qubein writes in, *How to Be a Great Communicator,*

> Those who lead the American workforce of the twenty-first century must learn to communicate with a variety of cultures. The workforce has changed because American demographics have changed. The predominantly male environment of the early twentieth century is gone. In its place is a colorful demographic brocade.

Qubein—himself an immigrant and now a highly regarded communications consultant—insists that today's leadership must find ways to bring this ethnic and cultural mix into leadership positions: "It is not just a matter of fairness; it is a matter of necessity."

As Hinz points out in *Communicating with Your Patients*, to be successful in dealing with a broad ethnic and cultural mix, physicians will have to become "aware of someone else's cultural beliefs, acknowledge that discrepancies exist between theirs and your own, and display an ability to meld the two." To lead a workforce that is increasingly diverse culturally will require continued commitment to a common goal, modern medicine, and great sensitivity to different styles of communication and to the nuances of behavior in more than one culture.

## The Common Language of Modern Medicine

The American system of health care enjoys one important advantage compared with the business practices of multinational corporations. Despite any cultural differences that may exist between you and the co-workers in your medical practice, you still share a common belief in the value of Western medicine. In fact, just because someone on your staff is of the same race or ethnicity as a particular patient, you cannot assume that the staff member will effectively bridge any cultural communication problems that you and the patient may be experiencing.

In Chapter 3 of *Communicating with Your Patients*, Hinz tells of one Spanish-American head nurse who, when translating for her colleagues, continually held back information about Hispanic patients' beliefs in folk remedies. She justified her decision by saying, "Patients shouldn't believe those things. I tell them that, and I don't translate what they say to the doctors…. This place is dedicated to modern medicine…. If I tell the doctors, they might think that I believe in that, too."

Although this nurse was eventually persuaded to share such information in the best interests of the patients, this anecdote points to the underlying fact that, no matter the culture, those who embrace health care as a livelihood have committed to a scientific point of view that often supersedes their personal origins. Generally, it is of great advantage that you and your staff share attitudes about what causes disease, what good patient care consists of, and the reliability and importance of tests and therapeutic drugs.

## High Context, Low Context

"Cultural differences begin as soon as communicators encounter one another," writes Christine Hinz in *Communicating with Your Patients*. How do we perceive cultural differences? These differences can range along a continuum of behavior that will be displayed far differently in the work environment than in the examining room.

In your examining room, you and your staff will be focused on eliciting information from a sick patient. In your daily interactions with staff members, though, you may find that staff members have notably different opinions about what behavior is polite, where a person should stand while conversing with another, when to show deference, how to address another person, and what topics are not proper to include in conversation. Many of these variations stem from cultural differences. In a well-managed practice, cultural differences will not impair medical care. Instead, differences in perspective can produce a broader understanding of patients' symptoms, expectations, and care.

In studying culture it is helpful to understand the distinction between *high-context* and *low-context* cultures. American culture is a low-context culture, which means that Americans do not assume a great deal in communication and in conversation. As Esther Wanning writes in *Culture Shock! USA, A Guide to Customs and Etiquette,* "As a low-context culture, we don't have many set routines for particular situations. Elaborate protocol cannot survive in a free-floating society. Formality seems undemocratic to us, and Americans dislike rituals of etiquette that recognize class differences. Our easy manners contribute to the fluidity of our society."

Wanning points out that it is easier for foreigners to participate in American society because our low-context culture makes it harder to make a serious mistake. American society is open to newcomers, and Americans themselves do not consider tradition sacrosanct or custom immutable. When you sing the lyrics, "You say tomayto/I say tomahto. You say potayto/I say potahto," you are actually making a statement about a culture to which many Americans subscribe. Most Americans tend to shrug off cultural differences, at least those differences with the Canadians, British, and Australians, on the assumption that people are all more or less alike. This attitude fits in with our democratic vision, but it can also cause Americans to blunder.

While low-context American culture may be easy to navigate, the lack of firm rules strikes some people as chaotic and threatening. The atmosphere in the office may seem very informal to them, such as the use of first names, the ease with which Americans reveal certain kinds of personal information, and the almost endless supply of birthday cakes and cookies.

Low-context culture may not seem respectful of legitimate differences: Are Americans really polite when even the English language seems to level people into one indistinguishable mass? Keep in mind that in English, we only use one pronoun, *you*, to address another person (*thou* having become pretty much obsolete). In French, there is a strong distinction between *tu*, reserved with family and friends, and *vous*, the pronoun used with persons who are less well known. If you lived in Paris, you might go to the same bakery for years and always address staff members as *vous*. To do so is a sign of respect. Remarkably, some husbands and wives use the formal form, too. The Italians go even further. The Italian language has four forms of address in the second person: *tu, voi, Lei,* and *Loro*. While Americans may think of Italians as informal, these distinctions are still observed, especially in writing. Italian culture is simply more high-context than is ours.

The recent bestseller, *Memoirs of a Geisha* by Arthur S. Golden, describes the high-context culture of Japanese entertainers who go through years of training. It is surprising that Americans should become so interested in a group of women governed by so many cultural assumptions and traditions. In Liza Dalby's *Geisha*, her remarkable study and memoir of her time as an apprentice geisha, she writes about how a geisha's hairdo and makeup are governed by conventions. The color and style of kimono depend on the age of the geisha, the time of the year, and other symbolism. (November is the month to wear vermilion over gray-green in a combination called maple.) The geisha's repertory of songs and dances follows certain traditions, too. Without careful study, an American invited to a banquet with geisha in attendance would not understand the subtleties whether or not he spoke Japanese.

While you may never be invited to a teahouse to dine with geisha, there are still situations that cause low-context Americans to stumble. Consider the following situations, many of which are daily events in an American office:

- *Naming customs.* Is Dr Wu's wife called Mrs Wu? Among Chinese women, it is not the custom to change one's name upon getting married. It is better for you to find out her full name, especially if your duties will call on you to introduce her to other staff members or colleagues.

- *Level of informality.* Do you sense that some members of the staff prefer not to be called by their first names? While Americans may enjoy being called Spike, Babs, and Jimmy at the office, in some cultures, nicknames and first names are reserved for the family. You may think that titles do not matter, but in many cultures, they are important indicators of status and respect. If Dr Shahidpour's husband is a professor, you may be more polite introducing him as Professor Shahidpour rather than as plain Reza.

- *Appropriate times to shake hands.* Europeans seem to shake hands more often than Americans do. Americans tend not to shake hands with people whom they see regularly, while some Europeans shake hands as a daily greeting.

- *Gift giving.* As much as Americans make a fuss about Christmas, gift giving is quite informal in the United States. In some cultures, giving or receiving a gift is a sign of obligation and deep respect. Reciprocation is a ritual, almost an art form. People from these high-context cultures may perceive the office grab bag as terribly impersonal.

- *Communication style.* In some cultures, it would be the height of rudeness to contradict a superior. You may find that there is little dialogue in some staff meetings. Do not chalk this up to lack of ideas or general shyness. Some people have been trained not to use a meeting as a forum to say whatever is on their minds. You may find that you get better information and advice from certain colleagues if you speak with them in private.

In *Culture Shock! USA, A Guide to Customs and Etiquette*, Esther Wanning makes an interesting point about oral communication, which she calls *style of talk*:

> Americans admire someone who thinks fast and always has something to say. Among friends, there's apt to be a lot of cheerful banter going on. This very volubility makes some cultures distrust Americans and consider them insincere. If someone has something to say about everything, how much could she really know? On the other hand, there are those—the French, for instance—who find Americans ponderous talkers.

Wanning does not believe the American myth of the cowboy of few words. She finds the nation to be peopled with relaters and socializers who have developed a low-context culture that requires them to explain more in conversation. The French, in contrast, value sparkling, allusive, and lively conversation, the product of a nation that sees itself as witty thinkers. The Japanese, however, have a slight mistrust of words, no matter how charming. Japanese children are taught that listening sincerely and relying on heartfelt feeling are more important in communicating with others than words.

Knowing that Americans were brought up in a low-context culture should help you in watching for signs of differences in cultural outlook among your staff members. You will have to decide how to accommodate the differences and even whether some differences may have to be glossed over to encourage unity in the office.

## Out of Many, One

It is important to recognize that there is more variety among health-care workers than in the past. Physicians need to adjust to these unaccustomed differences, much as American business executives must learn how to meet their Japanese counterparts properly, understand how their Turkish partners negotiate, and assess a Thai manufacturer's products and capabilities.

Begin by making all of your employees—regardless of skin color, gender, first language, or country of origin—feel welcome and comfortable in your practice. When it comes to your decidedly diverse staff of the future (if not the present), following are some basic practices and manners that may enhance your interactions:

- *Establish effective lines of communication and keep them open.* This process is a hallmark of all good physician-staff relations. Good communication may involve repeating information and checking to ensure that people have understood what you expect. Norine Dresser points out that it is polite in many cultures to turn down food and drink when they are offered, often as many as three times. Think of how different an American banquet is. If you turn down a plate being offered to you by the server, you could end up with no dinner at all. Be prepared to offer information more than once, too. It can be a way of building consensus.

- *Understand your staff's capabilities.* Americans pride themselves on running fair and democratic offices. Immigrants to the United States expect to be treated fairly at work, too, which means not being stereotyped by background or country of origin. The new nurse may be from India, but that does not mean that Hindi is her first language. She may speak several other Indian languages (which may be a bonus to your practice in providing patient care if you take time to find out). Also, make an effort to translate training and education so that you understand your staff members' skills. They may have special training in tropical medicine, nutrition, public health, or child development that is not required by American universities.

- *Learn how people hold their bodies, touch, and converse.* Understand what might offend and then avoid such behavior. In many cultures, good manners may not allow a man to touch a woman who is not his wife or a female relative. You may have to explain to new staff members what is allowed in American culture. On the other hand, in some cultures, people stand much closer to converse, touch each other more often, and hold hands or link arms as signs of friendship. Americans, though, stand rather far apart when talking and rarely touch or hold hands casually. Again, you may have to explain American habits to your immigrant staff members (and vice versa). A compromise level of touching may have to be agreed upon (especially in light of American sexual harassment law).

- *Learn what ways of expressing yourself are polite and acceptable.* Native-born Americans actually may be at a disadvantage here. Speaking English, a world language, Americans generally do not master other languages with ease. On the other hand, immigrants to the United States often speak English as their third or fourth language. People whose first language extends over a limited geographic area such as Lithuanian, Wolof, Amharic, Hungarian, or Tagalog often learn world languages such as English, French, and Spanish to widen their perspective and sources of information. Further, many Muslims, regardless of their native language, have studied Arabic, their liturgical language. For these reasons, many immigrants are already highly sensitized to polite and acceptable speech, appropriate written instructions, and correct grammar. Exposure to many languages does not mean, however, that everyone will understand the slogan, "Just do it!," or even consider it proper English. Be careful when using common colloquialisms, figures of speech, vogue words, or other vernacular terms and phrases.

- *If you want to learn more about the differing cultures of your employees, start by demonstrating a sincere personal interest.* Reinforce this interest by scheduling cultural awareness training or workshops for the entire staff. This requires some commitment. No one wants his or her culture to be treated as the flavor of the week.

- *Be careful when using humor.* Americans expect the icebreaker joke or witticism at the beginning of a class, seminar, conference, or sermon at a wedding. What they fail to remember is that most people attending a function have shared experiences and expectations. In fact, many people fail to understand humor, and senses of humor vary widely. Those jokes about people not getting jokes are based on fact.

- *Above all, never patronize and do not allow any disparaging slang or slurs to be expressed within the work setting.* Most Americans make an effort not to use ethnic slurs, and few offices tolerate them. Be careful when asking about someone's background. This is when people often are innocently patronizing. You may make a comment that you believe to be cordial, "China has changed a lot in the last decade." Your listener may be a Taiwanese with little regard for the mainland. The result is bewilderment.

## Change, Conflict, and Cohesion

The different personality types discussed in Chapter 1 are in part creatures of culture. Certain cultures have different styles, or approaches, to various communication issues. Some cultures have a low tolerance for conflict or confrontation. You may find Japanese or Indonesian etiquette to be complicated, but the purpose of such elaborate manners is to minimize confrontation and conflict. Employees from such cultures may find it offensive or disconcerting if someone raises his voice, for example, even if it is not directed at them personally. In some cultures, the truly powerful person does not raise his or her voice at all.

As mentioned in Chapter 1, the relater and thinker personality types tend to be uncomfortable with change. People from other cultures may be just as uncomfortable with change or risk at work, especially because they have already made the overwhelming decision to immigrate to the United States. If your practice is about to be restructured, employees imbued with this cultural bias may find it more difficult to adjust than employees who come from a culture predisposed to be flexible in the face of unpredictability.

The best way to manage change is through open communication. Be sensitive to different styles of communication. Encourage employees to bring their concerns to you, whether in staff meetings or in private. Building better relationships among staff members through open communication leads to greater staff cohesion, and more cohesive organizations weather change better.

## Religion and Diversity

American society has been characterized by religious diversity since its founding. Roman Catholics first settled Maryland and have since become the nation's largest Christian denomination. The Touro Synagogue, the oldest synagogue in the United States, was built by a Jewish congregation founded in 1658. And American Indian peoples preserve religious customs that originated well before the arrival of European settlers.

The diversity of religion and rituals in the United States leads to two important questions about religion in the workplace: Which religious practices and rituals should be accommodated? How should holidays be observed?

While religion is important to many people, the workplace has no obligation to foster religious belief. Nevertheless, religious celebrations such as Christmas and Easter and secular holidays such as Independence Day and Thanksgiving are part of the rhythm of the year and important social events. Striking a balance is important.

Accommodating religious practices may be relatively simple once you understand what the practices mean and how often the rituals occur. You should question staff members politely, discuss how their religious practice will affect the flow of work, and agree on a schedule or solution. For example, Sunday is not the Sabbath in all religions. Your Jewish and Seventh-Day Adventist staff members may ask not to work on Saturdays.

Similarly, Muslims are expected to pray at certain times of the day. If you have observant Muslims on your staff, you should become familiar with the times of the prayers and decide how staff members can reasonably be accommodated. Fairness is paramount when dealing with religious matters in a business setting. You may have to set out a policy about observance of the Sabbath or prayer at work. You should be careful to communicate and discuss your policy with staff members.

In a medical office or hospital, medical staff members normally wear uniforms. The uniforms identify the staff and are a sanitary measure—wearing street clothes in surgery risks spreading infections. Accommodating religious dress thus may pose some difficulties in a medical practice. The keys to handling such issues are good communication and fairness. You should make sure that you understand the importance of the item of clothing. Is it essential to the practice of the religion? Is it mainly a custom? For example, many Catholics wear religious medals, but they would be unlikely to maintain that wearing a medal is a central tenet of Roman Catholicism.

Fairness in accommodating religious practices and usages is especially important. If you allow Jewish men to wear yarmulkes at work, you will have some difficulty enforcing a policy that Muslim women may not wear coverings on their hair. The issue becomes whether religiously sanctioned head coverings are allowed, and you will have to communicate a fair policy to all concerned.

Most American offices and businesses celebrate the same holidays, and Christmas is the only religious holiday that is widely observed by closings of offices and businesses (Easter is always on Sunday). Ironically, not all Christians celebrate Christmas, and some denominations do not observe December 25 as the date for the holiday. You should assess the preferences of your staff. Jewish staff members, for example, are already used to a ritual calendar that does not conform to the Christian calendar. If you are not familiar with Jewish observances, you may want to discuss how to accommodate holidays with Jewish staff members. You may find that the solution is to offer a certain number of personal holidays so that staff members of different religious backgrounds have the option of taking holidays within their own traditions.

Finally, many events at work are commemorated with food. These celebrations range from cake and coffee on birthdays or candy on Halloween to more formal banquets on holidays or at retirements. Keep in mind that food and religious customs intertwine. Muslims and Jews do not eat pork. Buddhists often become vegetarians because they consider the butchering of meat to be violence against animals. Celebrating together is a great way to build bridges and enhance staff cohesion, but not if you serve foods that your guests cannot eat.

## Sexual Harassment

While much of this chapter has been concerned with the mix of cultures in the workplace, the issue of sexual harassment bears mentioning. The increasing importance of women in the workplace will lead to changes in corporate culture, which include how medical practices are run.

Sexual harassment is among the thorniest communication issues in today's workplace. Discussing sexual harassment makes some people squeamish, and some companies have been slow to communicate policies and train their employees to observe them. Nevertheless, while what is considered offensive may be open to debate, the problem exists. Further, although sexual harassment is often thought of as men abusing women, a member of either sex can in fact be the offender.

Sexual harassment law is based on laws against discrimination. Sexual harassment is seen as discriminatory and as interfering unreasonably with a person's work performance. Sexual harassment law is not an attempt to impose a certain kind of etiquette at work. Instead, sexual harassment law arose because people found that fellow employees were abusive and that often managers turned a blind eye to inappropriate touching, outrageous demands, and demeaning language.

The courts have defined two forms of sexual harassment. The first is sometimes called *quid pro quo sexual harassment*. Typically, the person making sexual advances implies that an employee must offer sexual favors to obtain a promotion, a contract, or other benefit—or just to keep his or her job. This is the most direct form of sexual harassment.

The second kind is called *hostile-environment sexual harassment*. In *What Every Manager Needs to Know about Sexual Harassment*, Darlene Orlov and Michael Roumell give this definition:

> In its most basic form, hostile-environment sexual harassment usually involves a situation where the workplace is replete with sexual comments, innuendoes, jokes,

inappropriate touching, or other degrading or abusive conduct of a sexual nature that is repeated and continuous over a period of time, becoming so bad that the average or 'reasonable' person finds it intolerable.

What these authors are describing, a workplace "replete with sexual comments, innuendoes, jokes, and inappropriate touching," is a workplace where communication has gone seriously wrong. Many persons or companies that end up being sued in a sexual-harassment case could have avoided creating an atmosphere conducive to harassment and lawsuits by focusing instead on enhancing the flow of communication, minimizing conflict, and building staff cohesion.

## Searching for Common Ground

In this chapter, we examined a major change in the American workforce—its increased diversity—and how this change affects communication within a medical practice. Having people of different backgrounds working together in a medical practice is not a recipe for conflict. Diversity is, however, best managed by great attention to communication. Those in positions of authority have a responsibility to make their messages understood. They also should make every effort to listen intently to what their diverse staffs are saying.

## Bibliography

Dalby L. *Geisha*. New York, NY: Vintage; 1985.

Dresser N. *Multicultural Manners: New Rules of Etiquette for a Changing Society*. New York, NY: John Wiley & Sons; 1996.

Hinz C. *Communicating with Your Patients: Skills for Building Rapport*. Chicago, IL: American Medical Association; 2000.

Golden, A. S. *Memoirs of a Geisha*. New York, NY: Random House; 1997.

Orlov D, Roumell M. *What Every Manager Needs to Know About Sexual Harassment*. New York, NY: AMACOM; 1999.

Qubein N. *How to Be a Great Communicator: In Person, on Paper, and on the Podium*. New York, NY: John Wiley & Sons; 1996.

Wanning E, *Culture Shock! USA, A Guide to Customs and Etiquette*. Portland, OR: Graphic Arts Center Publishing Co.; 1991.

## Web Sites of Interest

Career Exposure's Web site, "Honoring Diversity in the Workplace," includes links to dozens of organizations and companies concerned about minority and women's issues: www.careerexposure.com/diversity.html.

9to5 National Association of Working Women offers advice to men and women on workplace issues, including sexual harassment: www.9to5.org/index.html.

# Part II

# Building a Better Medical Practice through Better Communication

"And about whatever I may see or hear in treatment, or even without treatment, in the life of human beings—things that should not ever be blurted out outside—I will remain silent, holding such things to be unutterable...."

Excerpted from the Hippocratic oath, translated by Heinrich Von Staden.

# Chapter 4

# Positive Leadership: Understanding Yourself and Others

You value staff cohesion and teamwork. You are seeking to minimize conflict and to encourage staff members to work independently. How do you accomplish all of these great goals? With leadership.

Ironically, collaboration and cooperation within an organization rely on leadership to shape the group effort and direct that effort toward a goal. As Maxine Pollock and Jean Kouris write in *Smart Practices: Success in a Changing Environment,*

> A well-run practice has strong leadership. Although well-developed policies and pro-
> cedures and a highly skilled staff are essential, they alone are not enough. It is a
> strong leader who creates a vision for the staff; who understands that, in a successful
> practice, there must be synergy between the organization and the employees; who is
> able to articulate the philosophy and goals of the organization and uses them to guide
> others; and who provides the motivation for staff to do their very best.

Four characteristics of effective leaders emerge from Pollock and Kouris's definition. These skills, which are learned rather than in-born characteristics, bear repeating. A good leader:

- creates a vision for the staff.
- fosters cooperation and a sense of unity of purpose among employees in an organization.
- articulates the philosophy and goals of the organization.
- provides motivation for staff members to do their best.

This chapter focuses on these four techniques of enhancing life in the organization. To learn to apply these skills, though, a leader must make a self-assessment, which is often the toughest part of the job.

## Know Thyself

The oracle at Delphi was the religious center of the Greek world. It consisted of a sacred road, treasuries, a temple complex, and the oracle itself. One of the most famous inscriptions on the oracle was the seemingly simple advice, "Know thyself." This charge, "Know thyself," was one of the great themes of Greek civilization, and through our classical inheritance, it still resonates in modern life. To the Greeks, knowing oneself meant knowing one's own qualities and where a person stood in the world. Because the Greeks prized action, knowing oneself also meant understanding how to behave well and how to put one's ideas into effect.

The Greek idea of self-knowledge still dovetails with modern ideas of leadership. Roger Reid and Alys Novak, authors of *User-Friendly Psychology for Managing Your Medical Practice*, apply this central idea to underscore principles of management and leadership. They believe that knowing oneself poses a challenge to those responsible for guiding a modern medical practice: Do you know your own strengths and weaknesses? Can you objectively identify your own needs, motives, attitudes, values, preferences, and style? If you cannot be objective about your own strengths, weaknesses, attitudes, and needs, you will not be able to accurately assess such qualities in your staff.

As an exercise, divide a sheet of paper in two by drawing a line down the center. In one column, list your strengths. In the other column, list your weaknesses.

How do your strengths fit in with the needs of the organization? You may want to look again at the personality types described in Chapter 1. Which of the many qualities of the types serve your organization best? In general, leaders of medical practices should be committed to patients, enthusiastic, methodical, perceptive, flexible, and highly verbal. As good communicators, they will know how to interview patients, give clear directions to patients and staff, offer reasonable advice, and speak to people appropriately, in sympathetic language that their listeners can understand. A good leader also serves as an example—by working hard, displaying a sense of purpose, embodying the organization's vision, working well with others, and showing good judgment. Physicians who are good leaders give patients a feeling of confidence in both the physician and in the staff members.

What weaknesses will hinder your performance? Chapter 2 examines criticism and conflict. How many times have you heard stories of the brilliant lawyer, judge, psychiatrist, or management consultant who could not keep a staff? In many cases, leaders in highly specialized professions have few weaknesses in their training or mastery of the subject matter. Their many former employees will admit how thoroughly their former bosses knew courtroom procedure, negotiation, new-business startups, or the latest surgical procedure. Nevertheless, these leaders' weaknesses show up—often in how they offer criticism and how they handle conflict. Sometimes, our weaknesses are the down sides of our strengths: The brilliant negotiator of business deals may waffle with staff members or wear them down with endless minutiae and wheedling. The courtroom lawyer who argues so eloquently on behalf of clients may prove argumentative and carping with staff.

Because you may have found it awkward to write up a list of weaknesses on a sheet of paper, you understand how hard it is to be objective from day to day about one's shortcomings. Keep in mind that a leader's shortcomings are always on display: You have your back to your followers.

Finally, do you know what you don't know? How well do you know the full scope of your role and position? Many otherwise excellent managers and supervisors meet their downfalls by assuming that certain aspects of an organization are not under their purview. Physicians, though, can expect to be fully involved in the running of their practices. If you wrote down that one of your weaknesses is "impatience with detail," you may have to raise your level of tolerance.

## Creating and Communicating a Vision

Leadership involves developing a vision. Leadership also entails expounding a vision and campaigning for it, say the authors of *User-Friendly Psychology for Managing Your Medical Practice*:

> It involves keeping the vision alive as a beacon to guide the forward movement of your organization. It means not only being part of the executive team that shapes a common mission/vision for the entire organization, but also being a key player in shaping and articulating the vision for a department…. Most of all, it means making sure it happens through teamwork and empowerment.

Your vision is central to how the practice is structured and how it operates day to day. The vision is usually written down as a mission statement, which lists the purposes, goals, and values of the organization. As you begin to expound your vision and as you prepare to lead staff members in a certain direction, you should be aware of your leadership style.

In *Smart Practices: Success in a Changing Environment*, Pollock and Kouris describe four styles of leadership. Think about which style of leadership you lean toward. Then consider how leaders portraying different styles would disseminate their visions and encourage staff to buy into that vision:

- *Exploitative autocratic:* Highly directive and extracts performance without providing rewards. This is the least effective style for long-term employee motivation.

- *Benevolent autocratic:* Highly directive but rewards performance.

- *Participatory:* Encourages employee involvement in decision-making and exchange of ideas.

- *Democratic:* Encourages employee involvement and mutual agreement in all activities and decisions.

Of the four personality types, the director is most likely to favor the exploitative-autocratic style. Thinkers probably tend toward acting as benevolent autocrats, since they rely on their competence to justify their behavior. Socializers would tend toward participatory management, while relaters are probably the democrats of the office.

Just as your temperament is a blend of personality types, your leadership style is a mixture of these four types. After all, no one would ever work for or with an exploitative autocrat, and the number of staff meetings held in a totally democratic organization would swiftly bore people into finding new jobs. The situation often will govern your style.

Some decisions, especially related to medical care and patient relations, will have to be made in the benevolent-autocratic style. You may simply have to settle on a policy for how the telephone is answered and communicate that policy to all staff members. You will have to enforce standards of confidentiality. You also probably do not want all staff members freely offering their opinions about patients' conditions and prognoses.

On the other hand, as the practice of medicine becomes less hierarchical, it will evolve toward a more participatory and democratic atmosphere. There are many advantages to more participation and more democracy: Physicians do not have to make a decision on every issue because they can rely on the skills of their staffs. When employees understand the organization's vision, they can operate autonomously and shoulder tasks on their own. In a more open atmosphere, many areas seem to work with less friction, including assignment of work, work schedules, design of personnel policies, recruitment of new staff members, staff training, and internal communication. The public face—the face that your organization presents to patients—seems more cordial and welcoming, too.

## Fostering Cooperation

Cooperation is a subtle quality. We certainly miss cooperation when everyone at the office seems prickly and individualistic, but it is hard to instruct people in being cooperative. Cooperation is taught mainly through example. As leadership training expert Sally Jenkins says, "Employees always look to the leader first." The leader is giving cues about how to behave and how to treat others on the job. This cuing often takes place on an unconscious level, Jenkins adds, because of a natural human tendency called *mirroring*. Mirroring means that we reflect in our own behavior the mood and attitude of those with whom we are interacting. Jenkins explains, "It's what we do to be psychologically safe. We look to the top for our example."

Jenkins points out that everyone in a medical practice—from nurses to billing clerks to receptionists—will integrate the behavior exhibited by the physician leader into their own demeanor and conduct. "When a physician's tone is really negative, the whole structure falls apart," she warns. This ripple effect may result in lack of cooperation, increased tensions, high turnover, disgruntlement among those who remain, and diminished patient satisfaction.

Medical Group Management Association (MGMA) consultant Dick Hansen admits that consistently acting as a positive role model for one's staff to mirror is no easy task for today's heavily scheduled physicians. Even if the desire is there, serving as an example may get lost in hectic daily life in a medical practice. Hansen, formerly the manager of a multi-specialty clinic, stresses to his consulting clients that the physician must continually communicate his or her desire for a positive practice environment. Reiterating the message cuts through even a frenzied pace and reminds the staff of why they really come to work each day: "The patient is the most important thing we've got here. We've got to treat them with respect, kindness, fairness and civility." This message also reinforces your vision, and it gives the staff members a goal that they can work toward cooperatively—even as they try to deal with deliveries of supplies, insurance company paperwork, cancelled appointments, and unexpected snowfalls.

Hansen notes that his physician clients—many of whom are in governance, on boards, or shareholders—actively manage their efforts so that they can have the best possible practice within the parameters of health-care reform. "Even with the constraints of managed care, it is still the physicians' practice," Hansen stresses. "And they can do something about it."

Hansen thinks that the turmoil during the first years managed care was implemented has calmed. One result is that many physicians now want to work with the changes, instead of against them. Thinking has changed along with the system. Today physicians are "more holistic about problem-solving, rather than seeing only one problem at a time," as was more typical in the past. At the same time, the mindset of the contemporary medical practice is becoming more inclusive in its approach to staff issues, dovetailing both clinical and managerial changes in attitude. Relying on the management styles described previously to classify behavior, what we are witnessing is an evolution toward participatory management from a style that once was organized along the lines of a top-down benevolent autocracy.

## Communicating Goals and Philosophy

The lines of communication and responsibility are changing, too. What Hansen sees in his consulting business is that suggestions for improvement are passed from the board to the entire staff by means of managing partners and administrators. Also, with today's capitated patient population, there is more and more financial incentive for physicians to wisely use their staff at the mid-practitioner level. However, the operative word is *wisely*, which invariably involves improved communication, especially of the practice's goals and philosophy.

With the increasing demands on their own time management, more and more physicians now delegate preliminary patient care to nurse practitioners, registered nurses, and physician assistants. Beyond that, clerical support staff has a considerable impact on patient care, in terms of how staff members handle phone messages, appointments, greetings, insurance questions, and the like.

One shortcoming that Dick Hansen sometimes sees in the groups he consults is a failure to orient new staff. Following are some ways of avoiding this pitfall:

- *Hand out the mission statement.* When you are interviewing a candidate, hand out copies of the mission statement and other documents that explain the practice's goals and values. If a candidate seems uncomfortable with certain ideas, you may have a bad fit. It is better to know during the interview that you are incompatible than after you have hired the person. When a candidate accepts the job, also send these documents along with the letter welcoming the person to the practice.

- *Schedule training.* Some companies are too informal about assessing training needs and scheduling training. Employees may wait for weeks to attend a brief seminar on how to use the e-mail system. Start training on the first day. Otherwise, the employee who is left to himself will end up being trained haphazardly and may pick up bad habits.

- *Reinforce the central purpose of the organization.* No matter what their role, it is always a good idea to walk new staff members through the clinical area, so that they can better understand how a patient experiences a visit.

- *Indicate the goals for training.* If employees have to take three in-house computer seminars to operate the office's system, tell them so. Let them know how quickly they can proceed through training. If your organization is large enough that a schedule of seminars and courses is published, show the list to the new employee. Work out a training schedule.

- *Assign someone to help the new employee.* Another helpful technique is a mentoring, or buddy, system. This provides new staff members with one person they can count on for consistent assistance should they find themselves in a bind that could compromise patient care. The new employee and her mentor may also find other areas where training may be necessary.

The standard of all medical practices has always been detailed and thorough written policies and procedures. The time to acquaint oneself with their multifaceted instructions is not when one is frantic for an answer, but during the orientation process itself. In short, says Hansen, it is crucial to set up the right systems when training new staff.

## Motivation to Do One's Best

While training new employees is important, keeping all staff members energized is the purpose of motivation. It is helpful to have refresher courses for staff members who have been around for a while. Sometimes, staff members cling to certain out-moded procedures almost as traditions. Refresher courses are a good time to ensure that everyone is working the same way. They are also a good time to revisit the mission statement and to get staff to focus again on a shared vision.

The authors of *Smart Practices: Success in a Changing Environment* offer several tips for maintaining a high level of motivation among staff members:

- Appreciate the employee's efforts.
- Make work fun by ensuring that the employee fits the job.
- Offer opportunities for growth and accomplishment.
- Encourage employees to accept job empowerment—to initiate, plan, and carry out new ways of doing tasks.
- Pay adequately and competitively to attract and retain the best employees.
- Use incentives to reward employees individually or as group. Awards, a designated "employee of the month," or bonus days off show a manager's appreciation for employees.

Each of these tips relies on leadership. First, these practices should be included in your organization's goals and philosophy as ways of encouraging cohesion and minimizing conflict. They can become the basis for how your medical practice hires, treats, promotes, and rewards staff members.

Leadership from the physicians in the practice will be necessary to carry out these activities. Accepting job empowerment may be hard for some staff members, but they are more likely to rise to the challenge if you have set an example of cooperation, respect, and appreciation of their efforts. Likewise, staff members may take advantage of chances for growth if the organization values their efforts.

## Active Leadership

Recent changes in how health care is structured challenge physicians to reinvent their leadership styles. Shared decision-making is more effective in the patient-centered medical practice. Nevertheless, physicians still have to lead, especially in the following areas that build staff morale and excellence:

- Physicians should create a vision for the staff members.

- Physicians should foster cooperation and a strong unity of purpose among employees in an organization, especially by their example.

- Physicians should articulate the philosophy and goals of the organization.

- Physicians should provide motivation for staff members to do their best.

Each of these goals will call for continuous communication and active listening.

### Bibliography

Murphy M. "Setting the right example." *Unique Opportunities.* Nov./Dec. 1998.

Pollock M, Kouris J. *Smart Practices: Success in a Changing Environment.* Chicago, IL: American Medical Association; 1999.

Reid R, Novak A. *User-Friendly Psychology for Managing Your Medical Practice.* Englewood, CO: Medical Group Management Association; 1995.

### Web Site of Interest

W. Edwards Deming, considered the father of the revolution in quality control, promoted his ideas about managing staff over a long career. The W. Edwards Deming Institute has a Web site at www.deming.org.

# Chapter 5

# Management-Staff Communication: Empowering Your Staff

"More and more," Dick Hansen of the Medical Group Management Association notes, "MDs tell me they want to learn business disciplines as a tool for their medical practices, rather than as the be-all and end-all." One exercise Hansen has his clients do during consultation is to express the values of the group and what they expect of each other. Time and again, he notes, physicians say they want to learn how to communicate with their staff better.

Organizations in which communication is not a high priority are rife with uncertainty and inefficiency. As Reid and Novak write in *User-Friendly Psychology for Managing Your Medical Practice*, "When people do not have enough information communicated to them, they will attempt to fill in the gaps. You are familiar with the speculation and gossip that seem to pop out of nowhere. It can seem like people just search for something to worry about. Well, in fact, they do!"

In an atmosphere of uncertainty, staff members make assumptions. Assumptions can impair patient care, which is the main purpose of any medical practice. While physicians may be skeptical of applying business techniques wholesale to a professional practice, they have singled out communication as an issue of central importance in achieving high-quality medical care.

Assumptions are also time consuming. By communicating better, you reallocate the time given to creating assumptions into productive staff time. You also give people the information they can use to work autonomously—that is the power of information.

## The New Flattened Pyramid

Greater educational opportunities, the computer revolution, and the economic shift to the service industries mean that more people have access to more information than ever before. This ease of access has leveled the structure that authority traditionally perched upon—a hierarchy in which your power stemmed from what information you controlled.

The resulting new organizational structure still relies on knowledge, specialization, and training, but top-down communication is frowned upon as inefficient. Managing an organization no longer consists of issuing orders from on high. The flow of communication has to adapt to these new realities.

Business leaders have adjusted their thinking and their organizations so that the flow of internal communication adapts to these changes. Business leaders recognize that unbending resistance to change does more harm than good. Superiors no longer can simply tell subordinates what they want done, with subordinates only able to relate to superiors through layers of intermediate supervisors. Now, communication in the workplace means absorbing information generated throughout the organization. Every area within an organization is capable of creating valuable information and should receive all pertinent information. The more information is shared, the more it empowers staff and operations.

How much of this newfound attitude among business leaders transfers to your medical practice? Like managers of businesses, physicians know about change and have gone through what are mildly called "restructurings." Roger Reid, co-author of *User-Friendly Psychology for Managing Your Medical Practice*, points out, "HMOs had people flying by the seat of their pants. Some wanted to adjust to it. Others wanted to defy it."

Physicians' primary concern in the face of overwhelming change was with how managed care might impede their relationships with patients. At the same time, changes in the patient-physician relationship also have led to changes in the ties between physician and staff.

## The Golden Rule, and Not-So-Golden Shortcomings

Interestingly, today's changed attitudes in American business about lateral communication in some ways reflect the practice of medicine before managed care, when physicians had time to inform much-smaller staffs fully about every patient's case. Information sharing has special benefits in medical practices: By sharing information among staff, staff members act much the same as family members who are kept informed about a relative's illness. The family (and staff members) becomes more involved in the patient's care. Shared information gives them a stake in the outcome.

In *User-Friendly Psychology for Managing Your Medical Practice*, Reid and Novak encapsulate this experience in a golden rule: It is better to communicate broadly rather than narrowly except in true cases of confidentiality and sensitivity.

The golden rule implies a sharing of power, too. While physicians have shown themselves willing to follow this golden rule of communication, you should be aware that changes are still working their way through the health-care system. Some issues will remain unsettled. Changes in the structure of medical care have fostered some role confusion among various practitioners. The physician no longer delegates to a head nurse, who in turn delegates to subordinates. Today, specialized nurses share in the decision-making with physician assistants and even with physicians. The lines of authority and responsibility in patient care are not as clearly drawn as they were before managed care. The ideal of small staffs working as a whole—with all members knowledgeable about each patient's situation—may be a thing of the past.

"Managed care seems much better now than three years ago," says Reid, an industrial psychologist who consults with medical practices about how to create better management techniques. Gregg Easterbrook confirms this assessment in "Managing Fine" in a March 2000 issue of *The New Republic*, "Health has improved at the same time as costs have declined because managed care has forced doctors and hospitals to become more efficient; they may not enjoy this experience, but their increased efficiency serves society. Though many predicted managed care would cause health care rationing, for the insured, at least, there is zero evidence of it."

With managed care firmly in place, Reid and Novak's golden rule can make life in the new system easier. "Certain physicians have regular contact with their staff, almost on a case-study level," Reid says. "Those who don't share or explain make staff overly dependent. For example, if a nurse is in touch with a physician, that nurse can act with autonomy and authority. They don't have to repeatedly return to the physician with questions because they haven't been properly informed." Communication between physicians and mid-level practitioners works best when it flows back and forth readily, as when physicians allow such support staff more involvement in patient follow-up.

Physicians caught up in today's hectic environment and dealing with a rapid pace of treatment "may share [patient information] with staff, but not thoroughly enough," Reid continues. The unfortunate result is that medical staff often function "much like pieceworkers in a factory."

## Choosing the Right Channel

Reid offers this assessment of communication via technology: "So much is lost without face-to-face, voice-to-voice interaction." Is that always the case? Choosing the right channel (the means or genre of communication) helps the message go from the sender to the recipient more efficiently. Is face-to-face communication always the right way to communicate? Should you write off technology completely?

The following channels of communication are most appropriate to a medical practice (the advantages and drawbacks to each means of communication are highlighted).

### Written Communication

The main types of written communications in an office are memos, letters, annual reports (mainly from corporations), and internal newsletters.

**Advantages:** Everyone receives the same information in the same format. Memos and other reports can present detailed information succinctly. Internal newsletters help to build staff morale by highlighting good performance and personal achievements.

**Drawbacks:** The message may be sent, but you have no way of knowing if it was received: People often put written communications aside "to read later." Poorly written memos and letters often create confusion rather than resolving issues. Written communication is perceived as less warm than face-to-face communication.

### Spoken Communication

Typically, spoken communication is used during speeches, in structured staff meetings, and in more casual meetings and conversations on specific topics.

**Advantages:** The sender receives a great deal of immediate feedback. Presentation of topics can be flexible—and can be repeated if necessary. A well-done speech sparks enthusiasm in its audience.

**Drawbacks:** Spoken communication is more likely to be misinterpreted than written communication because there is nothing to refer back to. The speaker may be treated as an authority who will not entertain questions (a problem in staff meetings especially). Audiences lose interest quickly in poorly prepared speeches. The message cannot be as complicated as in a written communication.

### Visual (video) Technology

The content of videos ranges from speeches to dramatized situations to real-life footage.

**Advantages:** Videos are often used in training, where they can demonstrate specific techniques and behaviors. Real-life footage shows situations as staff members are likely to encounter them.

**Drawbacks:** Video may prove expensive to rent or to create. Rented videos may not reflect the circumstances in your office or the values that you wish to impart. Training staff members by having them sit and watch television may not produce the best results.

## E-Mail

Typically a component of a computer's Internet access, and powered by various software packages, e-mail is widely used for getting out broadcast memos. It is also used for exchanging brief messages inside and outside the organization and can also transmit computer files.

**Advantages:** E-mail is swift and costs little. Many people are good at solving problems through a brief exchange of e-mail messages rather than holding a face-to-face meeting. Broadcasting staff memos by e-mail saves time and paper. Two people can work on the same document by exchanging computer files, even if they work at different branches of the same organization. When used well, e-mail helps a staff member to work quickly and independently.

**Drawbacks:** Many people are not in the habit of checking their electronic mailbox often. Communication is informal and unstructured, and e-mail is notorious for exchanges of messages that escalate into conflict. E-mail systems are not confidential. Your message can quickly be forwarded to the wrong person or the whole office. Most people have become used to exchanging brief messages, sometimes lacking in needed detail.

## Voice Mail

Telephone answering systems are used to collect messages, and they also have the capability to send messages to several staff members at one time.

**Advantages:** People can leave brief and detailed messages in a format that is more personal than e-mail. For most people, the telephone has more priority over an e-mail message, a fax, or a memo, so they may respond to a voice mail more quickly.

**Drawbacks:** Voice mail is not good for gathering detailed information.

## "Eat-and-Talk" Meetings

Meetings tied into a meal are common in business. You are most likely to use or encounter eat-and-talk staff meetings at breakfast or lunch, "brown bag" training seminars (usually at lunchtime), and coffee breaks when staff members are introduced.

**Advantages:** Having a meal together often leads to a more cordial, less formal atmosphere. Lunchtime seminars and workshops are short, and staff members can usually fit them into their schedules more easily. Introducing new staff over coffee and snacks honors them and enables everyone a few minutes of socializing and relaxation.

**Drawbacks:** Meals often have to be held off site. Lunch, in particular, can be expensive, especially for a large group. Food is a distraction from the main message. Some people prefer not to attend because they consider mealtimes to be private time.

### Personal Notes

Usually, personal notes consist of a handwritten letter, a card, or a few lines on a sheet of memo paper or on a Post-It note. People often send photocopies of favorite cartoons, images, or quotations with a handwritten message, too. Further, it is considered good manners to write thank-you notes and messages of sympathy by hand.

**Advantages:** In a computerized era, people still value handwritten communications and perceive them as warm, spontaneous, and caring. A handwritten acknowledgment of a job well done can be a great morale builder.

**Drawbacks:** Handwritten notes usually are not adequate for detailed messages. They may be inappropriate for serious work-related messages, too. A handwritten note may imply a personal relationship. A note on a small sheet of memo paper or a Post-It note may get lost.

### Audio

Audiotapes or audiobooks are often used in training.

**Advantages:** Staff members can listen to the materials on their own rather than having to schedule a training class. Many people already listen to tapes and audiobooks during their commutes to work.

**Disadvantages:** It is hard to determine whether the staff member has listened thoroughly. Some people have no access to tape players. Others resist the technology.

### MBWA, or 'Management by Walking Around'

MBWA is a form of information gathering and communication advocated by Tom Peters. Tom Peters is a well-known management consultant known as a vociferous proponent of high-quality work in an unstructured atmosphere. MBWA is just what it says: Managers gather information by keeping in close contact with their staff members rather than staying in their offices.

**Advantages:** The give-and-take of casual conversations often sparks great ideas and insights. Barriers between different staff levels are broken down, which enables power and communication to flow in all directions. The manager can stay in touch with the tone and atmosphere of the office. Small problems may be solved quickly and informally.

**Drawbacks:** Sometimes, people like to be left alone to do their work. Some staff members will not participate in informal exchanges and prefer a more structured meeting to discuss their ideas and views.

Finally, the fax machine may not be all that helpful in internal communication, but it is still handy in many situations, especially in communicating with patients. The great virtue of the fax machine is that you can send copies of documents almost anywhere in a matter of minutes.

## Let Go and Communicate

"When you communicate *instructions* to your employees, you are limiting their latitude to respond," says Nido Qubein, author of *How to Be a Great Communicator*. "When you communicate *information*, you are expanding their latitude to respond." Giving staff members latitude to respond allows them to respond to situations creatively, thus empowering them.

Another drawback that Qubein sees are too many "stifling layers" of management that can impede communication from subordinates to superiors. If someone must filter through level upon level of supervisors to deliver a message, he would be lucky to make it to the top at all.

Medical practices are susceptible to the communication drawbacks that stem from too many specialized functions. It comes with the territory, because practices are specialized, as are the staff members within practices. If people are trained to define their responsibilities narrowly, "they have little understanding of the overall process," says Qubein. "Therefore, they might not recognize and pass along information that might be highly beneficial to management." An approachable manner on the part of physicians can encourage all staff to speak up when necessary. This is true of communication related to patient care as well as administrative issues.

But, *don't kill the messenger*. While this may seem like an obvious point, in many instances, the person who has to deliver bad news is blamed for it. This is a tendency that most managers find themselves having to control. Unfortunately, anytime a messenger is blamed, it puts a damper on the free flow of information in an office. If you get a reputation for not being able to handle bad news well, you will never receive any—and thus will be unable to manage your practice. At budget time, you may not want to hear that an expensive yet better computer system would be beneficial. Would you rather keep losing secretaries to the practice down the street that uses such a system?

In short, any way that you—the physician leader—can enhance the communication flow will only help your practice. This may be through more formal channels such as the employee newsletter, weekly meetings, or the suggestion box. You may also use informal means, such as taking "one or two minutes for interaction with staffers on occasion," as consultant Dick Hansen suggests. "This can be a real challenge in large practices," he acknowledges. "But it demonstrates the importance you place on treating others as human beings, not as interchangeable cogs in the wheel."

Both clinical and administrative support staff are privy to valuable patient information (which is why Tom Peters believes so strongly in MBWA). How many times do patients unload their concerns on the first available listener? It is important that you can learn from your scheduling receptionist that Mrs Braga was crying from anxiety over her recent visit to the cardiologist for heart-related pregnancy complications.

## What Helps the Practice Helps the Patient

Perhaps nowhere is interdependence among staff members more important than in a medical practice, where lives are at stake. In *User-Friendly Psychology for Managing Your Medical Practice*, Reid and Novak caution physicians and administrators that staff have a tendency to perceive their own woes also as the patients' woes. In other words, staff may believe, "When you are not taking care of me, you are not taking care of the patient."

One way to avoid this lament is to follow Dick Hansen's recommended ways to set a positive tone in your practice. One strategy is to "Take time to figure out how you can make your staff feel appreciated. Professionals of all stripes are often surprised to learn that even small gestures of appreciation can be meaningful to employees—even though these same leaders readily admit they appreciate such gestures themselves."

## Managing Stress

Often overlooked in the heat of continuing change, staff morale can become a casualty. Physicians may assume that everyone will simply carry on like troupers. They may—until the stress overwhelms them.

"Stress particularly is a factor for health care workers, as it is in any helping profession," Reid and Novak state in *User-Friendly Psychology for Managing Your Medical Practice*. "The strain of constantly being faced with human needs that often cannot be solved frequently leads to major stress incidents and burnout. And stress is directly correlated with change. The moves toward improved empowerment, teamwork and communication will help significantly with stress management."

Stress can contribute to the kind of human error that the medical community constantly strives to prevent. Staff members under stress have the natural tendency to focus on the stress itself, which means that they are not as attentive to the needs of their patients.

Physicians and other personnel are now encouraged to communicate with each other more about their patient-care activities to reduce the margin for error. Teamwork calls for better communication with all involved, and a team that works well together can lessen the stress each member experiences.

Keep the following issues in mind as you look for situations that cause stress and and as you try to relieve causes of stress:

- Be aware of your own communication style and its effect on others.
- Monitor potential sources of conflict and defuse conflicts in their earliest stages. (See Chapter 2.)
- Communicate through the appropriate channels.
- Communicate often, thoroughly, and cordially. Invite responses, and accept them graciously.
- Understand your staff members as individuals. Learn what kinds of situations cause stress for each of them.
- Help your staff members to find coping mechanisms.

Reduced stress on the job improves efficiency and productivity, and it also enhances well being. This calmer manner is conveyed to the patients and, in turn, fosters the patients' well being.

Finally, think creatively about outlets for stress. The desired outcome is to reshape draining emotional tension into energizing productivity. By anticipating how various staffers might react to a stressful situation, you can intervene and prevent them from feeling overwhelmed. By doing so, you promote a sense of individual control and confidence among them that may eliminate or lessen the stress.

## Stress Prevention Through Communication

One source of stress is dealing with potential emergencies such as power outages, computer breakdowns, short staffing, and unruly patients. Good communication also comes into play when planning for staff, as well as practice, exigencies. Feeling on top of things allays most stressful situations. For example, administrators can get staff involved in "what-if" scenarios and encourage supervisors to develop staffing contingency plans in case of unforeseen complications. Invite risk management agents to speak at a staff meeting. Ask computer experts to assure staff about backups and virus protection.

Above all, assume a leadership role in alleviating the stress factors in your practice. Would you want your patients to take on unhealthy levels of stress? So why should anyone in your practice—including the physicians—tolerate undue stress and end up with an ulcer?

In short, according to Reid and Novak in *User-Friendly Psychology for Managing Your Medical Practice*, through improved communication, both physicians and staff members can learn to prevent certain stressful situations through preparation and planning; take charge of how they cope with "uncontrollable" situations that cannot be foreseen; and use built-in support systems prepared for them by management.

## Giving Up Power to Gain Leadership

In this chapter, the discussion focused on the hows and whys of physician-staff communication. In the new atmosphere of managed care, the traditional top-down communications style has become obsolete. It has been replaced by sharing of information and a greater emphasis on continuous exchange of information and constant flexibility in handling patient care. Greater access to information also means that there are now more channels of communication. Physicians have more means of communicating with staff at their disposal than they did even ten years ago. By communicating more, and more effectively, physicians can also become better managers who are more able to handle stress, conflict, and new opportunities. The result is an empowered staff that works independently, efficiently, and with great professionalism.

## Bibliography

Alessandra T, PhD; Hunsaker P, PhD. *Communicating at Work.* New York, NY: Simon & Schuster; 1993.

Easterbrook G. "Managing fine." *The New Republic*; March 20, 2000.

Qubein N. *How to Be a Great Communicator: In Person, on Paper, and on the Podium.* New York, NY: John Wiley & Sons; 1996.

Reid R, Novak A. *User-Friendly Psychology for Managing Your Medical Practice.* Englewood, CO: Medical Group Management Association; 1995.

Murphy M. "Setting the right example." *Unique Opportunities.* Nov./Dec. 1998.

## Web Site of Interest

Tom Peters's Web site looks more like an advocacy group's home page than a business consultant's site, but you can judge for yourself by visiting www.tompeters.com.

# Chapter 6

# Creating a Collaborative Medical Team

## Bringing Competing Interests Together

Moving away from the older, top-down style of management—which managed care made obsolete—entails more than restructuring. To change from a rigid hierarchy to teams requires thinking about what *teams* are and how they should function.

In their book, *User-Friendly Psychology for Managing Your Medical Practice*, Reid and Novak point out that teams are characterized by a common mission, vision, values, and goals. These aspirations are then put into action by working together. Likewise, leadership of the group involves working together. In fact, leadership of a team is participatory, with direction of the team shifting depending on the person's functions and the needs presented by the situation.

Identifying values and generating a vision cannot be done in the old top-down management style anymore either. In *The Platinum Rule*, Tony Alessandra and Michael O'Connor "dispense" with the Golden Rule because it places limitations on how to communicate with others and, consequently, how to set goals, work in teams, and create a vision:

> Following the Golden Rule literally—treating people the way *you'd* like to be treated—means dealing with others from your own perspective. It implies that we're all alike, that what I want and need is exactly what you want and need. But of course we're not all alike. And treating others that way can mean turning off those who have different needs, desires, and hopes.

In effect, according to Alessandra and O'Connor, the old way of doing things created a hierarchy of needs and desires. The people at the bottom of the pyramid may have been treated well, but their needs and aspirations were not allowed to shape the organization.

Teams are not a panacea, and invoking the word *teamwork* does not mean that you suspend managerial judgment. As Alessandra and O'Connor point out:

> One of the reasons for the spotty track record of work groups is that we're generally naïve about them. Too often we assume that a group can automatically be a team.

We act as if we can just order a good group from Purchasing, and so we opt for an off-the-rack model instead of designing one that will best do the job.

Alessandra and O'Connor are particularly concerned with team building. If you apply their platinum rule to team building, you will focus on each staff member's needs, goals, communication style (see Chapter 1), and management style (see Chapter 4) as you create work groups. Because a team has participatory leadership, every member's management style should be assessed. Each member must be capable of leading the team, and less experienced members may need some skill building and coaching.

Team building is more than a matter of bringing people together and hoping that they can get along. You should take people's differences, strengths, and backgrounds into account. Once you have done so, you can put in place the three goals for productive teams that Alessandra and O'Connor identify (listed here):

1. The team members and you will be able to assign projects to those staff members likely to do them well.

2. The team will be able to "sustain a cooperative climate in which each person can gain genuine respect and recognition."

3. The management of the medical practice (in which you are likely to participate) can "customize work groups to get the best results in the most efficient, satisfying manner."

This chapter focuses on case studies of how two group practices were able to put systems in place to work effectively toward these goals: Prevea Clinic, a large multi-specialty practice in Wisconsin; and San Dimas Medical Group, a smaller group practice limited to obstetrics and gynecology in California. Both have had to make changes in the structure of the practice and in how they do business. Both practices have also found that working with highly motivated teams has led to better internal communications and, therefore, better medical care.

## Out with the Old at a Large Practice: Prevea Clinic Services

Prevea Clinic Services—the result of a January 1, 1996, merger—is "just getting its feet wet" with many new approaches toward better management through improved communications. Headquartered in Green Bay, Wisconsin, Prevea Clinic Services is an example of a large practice and is also an organization committed to change. Ron Menaker, Executive Vice President of Prevea Clinic, believes that Prevea's future promises even "more opportunities to evolve."

"I don't think there ever was true 'authoritative' rule, although some people may think there was. Leaders are identified by their followers," says Ron Menaker on the more traditional approach to physician-staff interactions. Menaker's views on practice management reflect the beliefs of virtually the entire 127-person staff.

Menaker points out that learning a new way of thinking is not the hard part. "The hard part is forgetting the old stuff. We *need* standardization," he continues, "although that's challenging because MDs are not trained in standardization. They're trained in independence."

To foster collaboration, communication is integral to Prevea's organizational culture. Communication is complex, as Menaker acknowledges, "We're dealing with tradition and biases, such as our individual biases about just what is managed care. To me, managed care means *managing care* for patients."

With much talk these days about illness prevention, Prevea is taking action in a partnership among clinicians, administrative staff, and patients to promote patient health through preventive measures. One telling example of this partnership is the clinic's 24-page catalogue to help patients with their own health matters. The catalogue, offered as a free publication to patients, contains informative references and recommendations from reliable sources about a number of health matters.

This collaborative effort between Prevea's clinical and administrative staff is one manifestation of how the group's operations—and its communication systems—flow directly from its values, mission statement, and vision statement. Prevea's core values are health-care excellence, cost effectiveness, and people. These values form its mission statement, which Prevea translates into specific goals in its vision statement.

By keeping the focus always on Prevea's values, mission statement, and vision, Menaker strives to "coalesce the team," so that team members recognize that they have an opportunity to leave a legacy. That legacy is the "continuous improvement of the quality of patient care."

"We have to use business principles to run things, but we always put patients first," says Menaker. "With us it's not just talk. We take it to the next step by measuring patient satisfaction. This provides valuable feedback for each of our providers. But we also measure how satisfied our employees and physicians are."

Menaker notes that Prevea promotes communication between physicians and staff through a "communication culture" that is led by the physicians. For example, the in-house newsletter, *Prevea Press*, goes beyond typical house organs to encourage staff communication through physician involvement. "Our front-page story is always written by an MD—to set the tone of leadership," Menaker points out.

At Prevea, teamwork is a constant. "We have multiple teams. We have dyads [physician and nurse]. We have on-call teams. We have teams of specialists for our various sites. We also have the administrative-physician team. For too long administration has been referred to as a singular body. But physicians drive everything we do here."

Like Alessandra and O'Connor, authors of *The Platinum Rule*, Menaker believes that anyone who manages has to be realistic, and even somewhat hardheaded, about teams. Menaker concedes that you "can't talk about teamwork if you're ramming something down someone's throat, although sometimes that's necessary. Still, you must do it in such a way that he or she can still feel good about their role and contributions."

"We want to be the leading health system in northeast Wisconsin," Menaker continues. "But we must define that in organized ways to reach out to the community." To further that goal, Prevea has set up a community foundation. Prevea also offers a speaker's bureau that presents a variety of talks on health care and prevention, at no charge, to interested local organizations, schools, and businesses. Another community service is Prevea on Call, which answers questions about minor injuries, illnesses, and other health concerns 24 hours a day, 7 days a week.

## Focusing on the Organization's Purpose

Providing high-quality medical care is about creating, organizing, and advocating what a medical practice can be and how the practice can achieve what it sets out to do. Says Menaker, "We forget how to bring things back to, 'Why are we here?'" Prevea sums up its own reason for being with fundamental qualities that stem from its core values and imbue its sense of purpose. "These are management and leadership tools we use hour by hour, day by day, so that if someone says they need something done, it gets done," explains Menaker. Prevea fosters the following "management and leadership tools" or basic qualities: service, integrity, caring, trust, competence, and credibility.

Management guru Tom Peters and other business writers caution businesses to "stick to the knitting," to focus on what the organization does best—which is often what it was designed to do. Many organizations have suffered financial reverses by falling away from their original purposes and values. At Prevea, these six basic qualities and the organization's core values are constantly kept in front of staff members as aspirations. This focus keeps staff members committed to the organization's basic purpose.

At its annual employees' meeting, the group discusses what has happened at Prevea, what is happening now, and what is going to happen. The 1999 meeting inspired 192 ideas, which were passed on to management to implement. Note that like many successful organizations, Prevea takes time out from day-to-day work to go on retreat, where staff members can step away from their daily workload to assess their roles in the organization and Prevea's success at meeting its goals. (San Dimas Medical Group, described in the second case study in this chapter, also places emphasis on the need to go on retreat to gain objectivity in dealing with the practice's issues and planning.) Passing along 192 suggestions to management is also a good example of participatory leadership in action.

Menaker encourages his staff to consider new ways of thinking. "Don't use the word failure," he tells people. Instead, he recommends that they look at it this way: You did not get the results that you would have liked based on the actions you took. You simply have to try different strategies.

## Managing an Upside-Down Pyramid: San Dimas Medical Group

Peg Board is Chief of Operations at the San Dimas Medical Group in Bakersfield, California. She defines her job as pulling in feedback from everyone on staff, keeping the lines of communication open, and remaining upfront and honest with employees at all times.

"We've turned the pyramid upside down in our organization, so employees are at the top and things trickle down to administration," Board points out. In fact, it was the physicians on staff who implemented this management style. The physicians recognized that when administrators simply mandate, it is not an effective way to address or resolve a problem.

The two physicians who originally began this obstetrics-gynecology group 18 years ago had the philosophy that the medical group should be a "family" or team, recalls Board. To this day, the physicians who work at San Dimas Medical Group do not consider themselves better than the others on staff. She emphasizes, "We don't want staff to feel intimidated or fearful about expressing their concerns."

Once a month, the group shuts down operations for a mandatory meeting of all employees and physicians "to hear what's on the minds and [in the] hearts. Things are heard across the board, even if they can't always be implemented," she says. Also, the physicians themselves go on a retreat at least once a year. Sometimes these retreats are extended to include the front-line supervisors, those supervisors who act as team leaders in addition to their regular jobs.

Beyond that, Board enlists representatives from various disciplines throughout the medical practice to participate in standing committees about ongoing problems such as patient access. There are about ten such committees, whose goal is to "tweak things" for better results. One recent positive outcome was an improvement in patient access for non-urgent care—from previous waiting times of longer than 3 months to a current status of less than 14 days. Depending on the issue, standing committees meet biweekly, monthly, or quarterly, Board says.

Another recent management step to ease the flow of communication across physician-staff lines is the designation of one physician as staff liaison. This physician also serves on the executive committee, and her purpose is to bring employee problems to the administrative level.

Board points out that even what physicians may sometimes perceive as a clerical problem is often, ultimately, their responsibility. In other words, the lives of physicians and staff members are thoroughly intertwined. One such predicament involved the dictation process for patient-visit follow-up. An ad hoc committee was set up—often the best way to dispatch minor problems that ripple through the organization. After just a few meetings with four physicians and their medical assistant—who had come up with a relatively foolproof system—Board devised a tickler system of reminders to track that each letter is signed off by the attending physician before filing. As Board aptly notes, coming up with workable solutions serves both physicians and administrative staff.

## Use Teamwork to Raise Quality

The central idea of this chapter is how to create productive personal relationships—teams that provide high-quality medical care. It is no surprise that Confucius, who was highly attentive to interpersonal relationships, would offer advice that can be applied to contemporary ideas about teamwork: "Don't worry if people don't recognize your merits; worry that you may not recognize theirs" (*The Analects of Confucius*. W. W. Norton, 1997). Alessandra and O'Connor propose a similar philosophy in *The Platinum Rule*, which calls for focusing on the needs of the other members of the team. This new web of relationships is likely to prove stronger than the old top-down organization.

## Bibliography

Alessandra T, PhD; O'Connor M, PhD. *The Platinum Rule*. New York, NY: Warner Books; 1996.

Confucius. *The Analects of Confucius.* Translated by Simon Leys. New York, NY: W.W. Norton; 1997.

Murphy M. Setting the right example. *Unique Opportunities.* Nov./Dec. 1998.

Reid R, Novak A. *User-Friendly Psychology for Managing Your Medical Practice*. Englewood, CO: Medical Group Management Association; 1995.

## Web Site of Interest

To see how Prevea communicates with patients and the larger community that the practice serves, go to www.prevea.com.

# Chapter 7

# Harmony: Increasing Cooperation and Cohesion

Practicing medicine has always involved attempting to save lives and reduce pain and suffering. This unique set of skills—curing disease, delivering babies, monitoring health, advising patients, prescribing appropriate drugs and therapies, and even making terminal illnesses less difficult—is what sets the practice of medicine apart from other business and professional ventures. Ideally, this reality will help to create an elevated sense of mission among all staff.

## The Harmonious Team

If properly communicated and channeled, medicine's noble calling can foster cohesion and cooperation throughout the ranks of the highly specialized physicians and staff members in a medical practice. Chapter 6 focused on creating a culture that enhanced communication. The purpose of the communication culture in the two medical practices studied, and all of the various techniques that the physicians, administrators, and staff members used to keep communication flowing well, was to improve teamwork. This chapter focuses on specific techniques of building harmony within a team.

Musical harmony results from bringing different musical notes together in a larger composition. Harmony does not, then, mean *sameness*. As indicated in Chapter 3, contemporary American society is quite diverse. Diversity and difference do not inevitably lead to conflict; in fact, harmony results from brining differences together. In medical practices, differences in attitudes can be partly attributed to the differences in training, education, and status among various practitioners and staff members. The question facing physicians is how to bring all of these elements together into a strong and pleasant whole.

Certainly, even during the current restructuring of health care, physicians remain at the top of the pyramid. The communication and management skills that will shape tomorrow's medical environment, however, are not the exclusive talents of physicians. Communication and management skills must flourish among the entire staff if the goal of the medical practice is smooth operation and high-quality service.

Whether physicians choose to administer their own practice or to delegate administrative decisions to a professional manager, effective staff relations call for rethinking staff responsibilities. The article, "The Care and Feeding of Your Staff" from the *American Medical News* advises physicians, "Give employees much more input than they've had before. Then they will work to accomplish the goals of the practice" (April 22, 1996). In other words, to accept new responsibilities, staff members need as much information as possible. If the physicians take meaningful steps toward a genuine communication culture, the staff members will respond by adopting the practice's objectives as their own work goals. This process of "buying in" can result in a significant benefit—strong unity of purpose throughout the organization.

## Understanding Roles

To achieve high-quality patient care and satisfaction, individual staff members must be concerned not only with their separate roles and responsibilities but also with how patient care proceeds from them to the next person or department. Otherwise, the physician is handing the patient over to the unknown, with potentially serious consequences. The physician must be concerned most of all, as physicians' extensive training gives them an overview of how patients should be treated. Even if they are delegating authority over staff matters, physicians are still the patient's advocate and must monitor the quality of medical care—for the sake of both patient and staff.

Contemporary health care diverts more responsibility for patient care further down the line—to mid-level providers such as nurse practitioners and physician assistants. It has become even more pressing for physicians (either through their administrators or independently) to communicate the importance of this responsibility.

Dick Hansen, a consultant for the Medical Group Management Association (MGMA), says, "Physicians often have no idea what patients have been through before they get into the examining room." In his consulting practice, Hansen frequently finds physicians unaware of how their patients are treated by staff when setting appointments, during lab procedures such as drawing blood, or in solving routine billing and insurance issues. "I continually stress to the physicians that they've got to be responsible for the manner in which the practice is run, for establishing expectations of how patients are to be treated by staff," Hansen continues.

Establishing and communicating expectations is crucial, too, with receptionists and other clerical staff members who may never have the opportunity to witness for themselves how the physician interacts with patients—to see by example the tone physicians want to set within their practice. To avoid a gap in staff preparation, the medical practice should consider walking all staff members, regardless of their assignments, through a patient visit as part of their training, showing them examining rooms, waiting areas, forms, and other aspects of a visit as experienced by patients.

Understanding roles may involve actually creating and shaping those roles. The following three techniques are often used to define roles and clarify staff interactions:

- ***Creating job descriptions.*** Defining what it will take to do a certain job will clarify that position's role. Physicians, working with administrators, should prepare written job descriptions for the positions in the medical practice. Written job descriptions are usually somewhat optimistic—they list many more job responsibilities than the staff member may in fact have to perform. Nevertheless, written job descriptions also convey the organization's expectations. The physicians can express what the job entails, and the staff member understands as early as during the interview process what kind of commitment the job entails. Later, the job description serves as the standard for comparison during the staff members' performance reviews.

- ***Maintaining clear lines of authority.*** Another technique used to shape roles is to formalize reporting relationships. Traditionally, formalized reporting relationships have been part of the structure of most organizations. A staff member reports to a supervisor who reports to an administrator, and so on. As teams have become an organizing principle in many organizations, team members find that they, too, benefit from formalizing some of their relationships. Team members like to have clear statements of how they should interact and how communication should flow.

- ***Scheduling performance reviews.*** As mentioned, written job descriptions can be used in performance reviews. Written job descriptions provide an objective standard of achievement. They are also a basis for discussion. The staff member and the physician may agree that the staff member's role, as defined by the job description, is too limited. The staff member and physician can then agree on a new role. Staff members who rewrite parts or all of their job descriptions during a performance review are likely to meet agreed-upon goals, which they have a stake in. Creating one's own job is a great morale booster, too.

Job descriptions, lines of authority, and performance reviews may seem formal. They also create paperwork. On the other hand, even though teamwork leads to a looser atmosphere, people still like to know the ground rules. If everyone understands the ground rules, there is a better chance at harmony.

## Delegate, Delegate, Delegate

Strong administration no longer is about control but about empowerment and teamwork. Physicians who thought that management by control took a lot of work may find the initial steps toward teamwork and empowerment to be daunting. Harmony seems easy to recognize. Why is achieving it so time consuming and subtle?

To take a leadership role, physicians must communicate directly to the entire staff what their expectations of staff members are. According to Roger Reid and Alys Novak in *User-Friendly Psychology for Managing Your Medical Practice*, " . . . as medical practices strive for the most successful clinical and patient satisfaction outcomes, there must be a parallel focus on achieving the most successful staff outcomes as well. Without a solid foundation of empowered employees, productive relationships and effective teamwork, medical practices will not . . . survive the hurricane."

Accompanying this whirlwind of organizational changes are individual stresses and uncertainties that require attention. Even in the most stable work environment, the human factor inherent in any staff situation is a constant challenge. Because these human factors, too, require attention, you may have all the more reason to delegate management to a trained administrator.

Conceding to the expertise of another in staff matters does not lessen your authority as a physician. In fact, it often enhances your authority by freeing you to be just that—a physician. A good administrator navigates the changing winds of managed care and helps steer your practice toward a safe port for both patients and staff. As stated in "The Care and Feeding of Your Staff" in the *American Medical News*, "You don't have to always be captain of the ship" (April 22, 1996). Further, the article points out that giving up some authority is not always detrimental, "That isn't all bad, because if the ship goes down, so does the captain."

Just exactly what makes a good administrator, whether a physician or nonphysician? A good administrator is someone with an eye for talent and detail. Also, let's face it, a good administrator has an eye for trouble—in the sense that good managers anticipate what changes (whether internal or external) may disrupt the harmony of their organization. Good administrators are people-savvy and are deft at handling nonhuman resources such as furniture, office space, supplies, staff time, and parking spaces.

To promote harmony in a medical practice, you should look for administrators who display certain qualities and foster them in others. In *Communicating at Work*, Tony Alessandra and Phil Hunsaker recommend the following five qualities to lessen the likelihood of conflict and to build more harmonious relations:

- **Openness.** Openness means well-crafted communication with others and full discussion of all issues in a cordial atmosphere. Openness also means general approachability.

- **Empathy.** Empathy is the ability to know another's feelings and why those feelings arose. Empathy does not always require that you agree with the feelings and motivations, but it does entail a deep understanding of human behavior. If you have empathy with a staff member, you are less likely to feel that conflict will resolve your differences.

- **Supportiveness.** Supportiveness is one of those homely virtues that is hardly ever mentioned. How many times, though, have you felt abandoned because other staff members are distracted, the atmosphere hectic, the schedule packed from morning to night? Teams that work well consciously or unconsciously value the need for mutual reliance.

- **Positiveness.** More than one writer has remarked on how much cheap cynicism and bland irony have infiltrated human relations in the last decade or so. Putting a brake on this trend does not mean becoming a Pollyanna. Instead, positiveness in the workplace means taking the stance that people can accomplish what they set out to do by working together.

- **Equality.** Foregoing chapters have mentioned participatory leadership and a democratic management style. Equality leavens these styles of leadership and management. Equality also calls for each person in a team to recognize that the other members' opinions, decisions, and judgments are valid and worthy of consideration. Fostering equality will also mean flattening hierarchy.

It is probably no accident that all of these are qualities that team members should value and cultivate within themselves and in their co-workers. These qualities also make it easier for physicians and staff members to focus on a central issue in medical care, providing high-quality service to the patients.

## Using Service to Build Cohesion

"A physician has to demonstrate an attitude of service, so that the staff will do the same toward patients," says Dick Hansen, a consultant for the MGMA. This attitude of service may have been a given in the past, when medical practices were smaller and staffing roles more clearly defined. Now, settings are larger, more complicated, and staffed by an array of ancillary personnel, many of whom feel some role ambiguity. For example, the field of nursing is ever changing and increasingly specialized, not to mention all the specialties of all the others on your health-care team.

Indeed, as managed care demands that more patients be seen in shorter visits, even those among your staff's lower ranks may provide invaluable extra sets of eyes and ears for the time-pressed physician. For example, encourage your medical assistants to communicate with you if they note that the patient displays any signs of distress during routine preliminaries, such as limping when getting on the scale to be weighed. In addition, such open communication may enhance the medical assistant's sense of purpose within a highly stratified system.

Another way to use communication to enrich the job of your office workers is to explain how their tasks contribute to improved patient care. The secretary filling out forms may feel more motivated if he or she knows that this vital information contributes to outcome measures. The result of better motivation will be improvements in service.

Not only does a shared sense of responsibility for patient care contribute to motivation of support staff, shared responsibility also creates a sense of belonging to the team—rather than being a cog in the machine. "Knowing that you are involved together in fulfilling a vital mission helps people bond," say Reid and Novak in *User-Friendly Psychology for Managing Your Medical Practice*. This psychological gratification in turn improves employee retention and performance.

Conversely, today's fast-moving medical practice sometimes robs the more seasoned professionals on your staff of their sense of purpose—including you, the physician. Physicians and nurses whose training conflicts with the imperatives of managed care often experience distress over their new roles. In such cases, the empathetic ear and communication skills of a good administrator can help professional staff find ways to work within the new system and thereby alleviate stress.

No matter what the job title and tasks, participation by all staff in planning and implementing change will promote better results. For the busy physician, increased comfort with delegating authority is required. Yet the leadership role remains yours and yours alone, as the article, "Setting the Right Example," indicates:

> When a physician models an attitude of service, it spreads like a contagion throughout the practice. A physician who takes the extra second to greet staff members in a friendly manner, really listens when employees speak, and frequently expresses appreciation for a job well done is building a staff that will treat patients with the same caring and concern (*Unique Opportunities*; Nov./Dec. 1998).

## Removing Impediments

The harmonious office is characterized by certain qualities or virtues. These virtues, listed here, improve patient care and enable the staff to work well together:

- *Unhindered communication.* Staff members who receive a great deal of real input will learn that they are valued parts of the practice. Because information is so powerful, the well-informed staff member also feels a much stronger sense of ownership than the employee who feels left out.

- *Shared authority.* For some physicians, free-flowing communication is less of a challenge than is sharing authority and relying on others' expertise. In the past, physicians saw themselves as the most highly trained members in a medical practice—the sun at the center of the solar system. Now, however, physicians have to recognize the value and power of service, management, and the team itself.

- *Real delegation.* This quality obviously is related to the sharing of authority. If the goal is teamwork, delegation should be easier for physicians. All members of the team should be prepared to have work delegated to them and to delegate to others intelligently.

- *Attention to quality throughout the practice.* The quality revolution that began in manufacturing industries and that later spread to services produced remarkable changes. One of the most powerful ideas to come out of this revolution is that attention to quality is the responsibility of all employees. To enhance quality, though, the old top-down management structure has to be removed to enable better monitoring of performance. Newly empowered staff members do not need a rigid management structure. Instead, to produce the best results, staff members should have real power to effect change and build strong unity of purpose.

## Bibliography

Alessandra T, PhD; Hunsaker P, PhD. *Communicating at Work.* New York, NY: Simon & Schuster; 1993.

Clements B. "The care and feeding of your staff." *American Medical News.* April 22, 1996.

Murphy M. "Setting the right example." *Unique Opportunities.* Nov./Dec. 1998.

Reid R, Novak A. *User-Friendly Psychology for Managing Your Medical Practice.* Englewood, CO: Medical Group Management Association; 1995.

## Web Site of Interest

The Association for Quality and Participation emphasizes leading organizational change, creating a learning organization, and adapting to the New Economy. AQP maintains a Web site at www.aqp.org.

# Chapter 8

# Using Technology to Enhance Communication

"Communication issues are the heart of operations—and an integral part of management," says Elizabeth Woodcock, operations consultant for the Medical Group Management Association (MGMA). In her consulting practice, she often advises medical practices in ways to use information systems to enhance staff communications and patient care.

Woodcock sees three dependent variables that affect interactions among physicians and staff. The first is the facility itself; the second is its information systems; and the third is attitude. For those physicians who want higher productivity in their practices, as well as improved staff relations, rethinking their channels of communication is key. This chapter focuses on using technology to enhance communications. Admittedly, some of the suggestions are low tech (such as color-coding), but other suggestions involve taking advantage of the capabilities of computers and other new electronic gadgetry.

## It's True: Time Is Money

Physicians who insist on maintaining total control over everything that goes on in their practices often impede productivity. In her consultations with physicians, Woodcock underscores that time is a precious commodity. Time often is wasted when physicians will not delegate whenever possible.

"Staff utilization is the single most costly resource," Woodcock points out. A hierarchical mindset in a physician is not as productive, she emphasizes, because with proper written protocols, nurses and other mid-level practitioners can ease the patient-care process.

Free-flowing communication and a commitment to teamwork maximize efficiency. However, according to Woodcock, "It's up to the physician how they communicate that on a day-to-day basis." She suggests that there is a time for face-to-face communication and a time for alternate methods that do not squander minutes that add up to hours as people try to hunt down various personnel so that they can deliver verbal instructions. In addition to their value as time savers, these alternate methods also offer a risk-management bonus by reducing the communication breakdowns that strictly verbal exchanges sometimes lead to.

High-tech machinery and systems, in particular, have brought rapid and constant change to the office. Even if your staff members are computer literate, they may resist changing to a new computer system or learning new software. In *Smart Practices: Success in a Changing Environment,* Maxine Pollock and Jean Kouris suggest the following four-step process for building support for change:

Step 1: There must be a clear understanding of why change is needed.

Step 2: Create a shared clear vision.

Step 3: A "buy-in" is needed. The benefit of the change must be evident.

Step 4: There must be commitment and sponsorship from the top.

These steps apply to internal communication whether the change involves a different system of color-coding, a new telephone system, a decision to eliminate written memos, or the practice's e-mail etiquette. Good communicators and managers ensure that every physician and staff member involved understands the reasons for the change and how the new system or equipment will enhance patient care and improve workflow.

The buy-in is especially important. One of the best ways of getting people to accept new systems or equipment is to have them participate in the purchase. Staff members can read brochures and evaluate different models of machines or software packages. Participation enhances the feeling of ownership—and also generates excitement and acceptance of the change.

## Simple Ways to Stay on Track

If every communication does not have to be face to face, physicians should decide on the channels (and devices) that are most convenient and appropriate for certain messages. "Maybe it's because they have to deal with so much paperwork in their practice," Woodcock speculates, "but physicians seem to resist using paper to communicate with their staff." For some messages, though, paper is the most advanced technology needed. Woodcock recommends that medical groups create a printed, customized routing slip that lists their specialty's most routine procedures. Such a slip enables physicians to check off instructions for staff easily.

Besides indicating what procedure the physician has ordered, routing slips also can help with logistics such as which exam room is next on the schedule or when a patient is in the waiting area. Such routing slips can be combined with the charge ticket and therefore become an effective tracking system. Color-coding further improves this system, Woodcock points out, and is easily effected using the array of neon papers now available.

## Lights, Colors, Action!

Medical staff has always relied on understood signals to ease communication and streamline procedures. What operations consultants such as Elizabeth Woodcock recommend is to improve on these existing techniques. Lighting systems now available, for example, use colors in a flashing order to expedite patient care. These lighting systems are usually integrated into new construction, says Woodcock. Red lights might indicate to the nurse that the patient needs lab work, for instance. Yet even an intricate lighting system cannot convey the all-important detail that a routing slip can, points out Woodcock. "The nurse may know by the red light that the patient needs lab work, but the routing slip tells staff what type of lab work." This simple paper system is an invaluable supplement to high technology.

Other color-coding methods often used in medical practices are flags on doorframes to signify useful information, such as that the patient is already in the examination room. These flags can serve as an extension of the chart-positioning method so often used. Typically, a chart placed sideways indicates that the patient exam is completed. A chart flipped upright means that the patient is ready to be examined. Another possibility that Woodcock suggests is to use color-coded clips to alert staff to written instructions.

## Electronic Gadgets with a Purpose

The revolution in computer hardware and software has created an array of devices that ease the flow of communication in the workplace. The five devices most likely to have made an impact on a medical practice are computers, e-mail capability, access to the World Wide Web, facsimile machines, and hand-held computers. All of these devices are readily available. When purchasing a new machine or system, though, it is important to think about how its use can enhance communication. While we sometimes call fax machines and hand-held computers *toys*, they in fact can have a beneficial impact on communication at the office.

While medicine is increasingly high tech, attitudes toward electronic equipment still vary. The recent Year 2000 scare was a good example of how much people misunderstand machinery and distribution systems. So even though your staff is familiar with MRIs and electronic thermometers, you may find yourself explaining why e-mail is a useful way of communicating in the office. If you need to do so, make your case for high-tech communication to everyone involved. Usually, a low-tech vehicle, such as a memo to all physicians and staff members, is the best means of getting the message out. Demonstrations help, too, as physicians and staff members can see how the machine or software package works rather than just receiving a manual to study.

## Computers' Immense Capabilities

Computers are everywhere, and computer literacy has become an essential skill unless you like typing messages on your old upright typewriter. Now that computers have proliferated in medical offices, how can they be put to work to enhance communication, ease the flow of work, and eliminate tiresome tasks?

Many offices do not take advantage of the capabilities of their networked computers. Instead of weaving a network of shared databases, software, and directories, some companies rig a series of isolated personal computers that have trouble talking to one another. Why have a network at all if you do not maximize the sharing capabilities among the computers? Shared directories enable staff members to organize their work better. Shared directories also let staff members share files, which means that they do not have to repeat work. Sharing directories and files may also lead to greater cooperation among staff members. In many configurations, members of a team or department have a shared or public directory where they can place files that more than one person will work on as well as a personal directory or drive where they can keep their own work.

The major objection to sharing directories is that people do not organize their computers alike. People who are highly organized are leery of having to work with a person who keeps everything in a single large directory named "Jim's Files." Your response should be to have teams set up protocols for their shared directories and files. How should files be named? Should all memos be filed together in a special directory of their own? Who should create templates for certain regularly used documents? These are all questions that can be hammered out in a meeting at the time that the shared directory is being planned and set up.

Keep in mind that determining access to files is another important protocol. Some directories will need password protection. Some staff members should have limited access to confidential files, and their passwords may not allow them into every directory. If you do put some directories off limits, you should explain to staff members what qualifications allow someone into those directories, and rules of access should be fair.

While shared directories and files can make work more efficient, computers' ability to transmit data instantaneously is a powerful tool for management. Networked computer systems can transmit patient status to the back office in nanoseconds, enabling staff members at the front desk to keep the rest of the office informed of patients' arrivals, whereabouts, and departures.

Currently, says Woodcock, the time lag between when a patient arrives and when nurses are alerted to that arrival is far too long in most medical practices. To protect patient confidentiality and save space, Woodcock proposes that a terminal be suspended above the nurses' station, with its screen readable only within the nurses' line of sight. Each time a patient is registered by the front office, his or her name, with an "A" for arrival, is highlighted on the screen to notify the nurses. To further ease communication with the clinical staff, the front desk also may enter the patient's chief complaint into the computer. Nurses, in turn, can then enter additional patient data for ancillary staff such as labs.

Another suggestion Woodcock makes is beautiful in its simplicity—and somewhat cheaper to implement: install a printer in the nurses' station. When the receptionist enters referring data during patient registration, those data go straight to the back office, where the charts are kept, as a printed document.

## Exploiting Electrons to Lower Stress

The personal computer gives access to e-mail and to Web sites through the use of modems, e-mail software, and Web browsers. While newspaper advice columnists may speculate about Internet addiction and offer cures, you are more likely to find that staff members do not exploit e-mail and its capabilities enough. E-mail messages are an excellent way of getting people together for brief meetings. E-mail messages can also be used to poll staff members—all they have to do is hit the reply button, respond to the request, and send their answer. Much of the information that once went up on corkboards as notes or into the occasional staff newsletter can now be sent swiftly to all concerned as broadcast messages.

Many companies, government agencies, schools, associations, clubs, and individuals maintain sites on the World Wide Web. A Web site normally would not be used for internal communications, but Web sites serve as another channel of communication between a company and its clientele. Medical practices are no exception. Because a Web site is a public document, it gives potential patients a chance to learn something about a medical practice before they make an appointment. Posting e-mail addresses at your practice's Web site will enable potential patients to make contact and ask questions. It may be best to post only your practice administrator's address, so that physicians do not receive unsolicited messages asking for free medical advice. If you funnel all e-mail inquiries through a central source, that person can forward the messages to the members of the practice who can answer any issues raised.

While some experts predicted that fax machines would become obsolete, they are too versatile to be left out of most offices. The fax machine is a convenient way of enhancing communication between different offices of a practice, as even long documents can be sent quickly to another location. You may also find that the fax machine is helpful in communicating information to patients because it sends an exact copy of the document. The main drawback of a fax machine is its lack of confidentiality. For example, you may not want to send even a blank form to a patient's business fax machine unless you can be assured that only the patient will see the form. On the other hand, many businesses now have fax machines, and the fax machine makes it easier for staff members to order supplies and equipment. The staff member can fill out the form and send it along rather than waiting to talk to the customer service representative.

Hand-held computers are the latest craze. For most physicians and other staff members, they will be especially helpful for creating schedules and reading e-mail messages. While hand-held computers can be used for calculating and word processing, many people find the screens too small for tasks involving a great deal of text. Nevertheless, these pocket-sized, powerful machines can be used to organize the day and to exchange information.

## Do You Read Me?

Another affordable way to improve staff communication is through the use of pagers. Pagers have become cheap. While most physicians associate pagers with being on call and away from the office or hospital, pagers can be used in-house to send simple messages. They can easily convey among staff which patient is where by entering the name along with "L" for lab or "E" for examination room, for example. Pagers may prove most helpful at such simple tasks, because the less expensive models do not display a wide range of information.

Pagers have some drawbacks, too. They can be loud and disruptive, and everyone has experienced, or heard about, pagers going off during a movie, play, or musical performance. For these reasons, some places of business, hospitals, and other institutions ask that they be turned off, which impairs their usefulness.

## Don't Forget the Telephone

With e-mail and the World Wide Web crackling through the telephone lines and onto computer screens, there is a tendency to forget the telephone itself. The telephone is still an excellent way to communicate with staff members individually. Conferencing features make group calls feasible and help if physicians and staff members work at more than one location. Finally, voice mail is a simple way to get a brief message to another person or a small group.

## Appropriate Channels for Efficient Communication

Chapter 5 focused on appropriate channels of communication within an office. Computerized technology, in particular, has brought speed and greater variety to these channels of communication. The five high-tech devices most likely to have made an impact on a medical practice are computers, e-mail capability, Web sites, fax machines, and hand-held computers. Physicians and staff members will buy into technological change through open communication. They will then adopt new systems readily and use new machinery and systems to enhance communication.

### Bibliography

Pollack M, Kouris J. *Smart Practices: Success in a Changing Environment.* Chicago, IL: American Medical Association; 1999.

### Web Sites of Interest

As mentioned in this chapter, a number of medical practices maintain Web sites to help patients learn about their services. Following are a few sites to consult. (Listing here is not an endorsement.) Each has a slightly different approach to how it offers information. The Katzen

Eye Group, for example, even includes anatomical images so that patients understand how their eyes work.

Prevea Health Systems, www.prevea.com

GEM Care, www.gemcare.com/index.htm

Northwestern Memorial Hospital, www.nmh.org

Mayo Clinic, www.mayo.edu

Katzen Eye Group, www.katzeneye.com

Dartmouth-Hitchcock Medical Center, www.hitchcock.org

# Chapter 9

# Morale: Building a Positive Communication Climate

In the last decade, many articles and books have been published about innovation, quality control, productivity, "reengineering the organization," and "management by objectives." Morale is a more elusive topic, but morale also happens to be the lifeblood of an organization. Positive staff morale is what brings people to work willingly each day, what gets them through stressful situations, and what enables them to overlook minor inconveniences. Employees with high morale may be enthusiastic, disciplined, reliable, cooperative, resilient, and creative.

When morale is low or negative, those same employees may drag into work, have little tolerance for stress (or patients), squabble about minor inconveniences and lapses, and communicate poorly. Morale is directly tied to communication. Poor communication has wide-ranging effects on an organization. A combination of low morale and poor communication can go so far as to bring operations to a halt.

It is not intuitively obvious that morale and communication are closely intertwined. Many managers would be inclined to say that morale is related to salaries or benefits. In fact, that is not the case. While everyone enjoys getting paid, morale and motivation are not strictly tied to the financial side of work.

## Making Morale a Priority

Morale derives from the free flow of information and the quality of personal relationships within an organization. This combination can be called a practice's *communication climate.*

The imagery of climate is apt, because a working environment can be sunny and calm or cold and stormy. You can test the climate of an organization by asking a few questions about attitudes and behaviors, such as:

- Do people on staff feel respected and appreciated?

- Do they believe that they can trust one another?

- Who takes the lead in setting a good example of interpersonal relationships?

- Is every effort made to include staff members in the flow of communication?

- Do suggestions for change move freely through the organization?

- Do all staff members believe that their opinions matter?

- Can you sense the esprit de corps?

- Has the practice determined what its core values are, and does the leadership of the practice continuously communicate those values to staff members?

Management trainer Sally Jenkins points out that knowingly or unknowingly, physicians set the tone for all of the staff members in the office. "Staffers instinctively view the behaviors exhibited by the physician not only as acceptable, but as desirable, and they integrate those behaviors into their own demeanor and conduct." Whatever your practice environment, the fact remains that the communications climate envelops your staff as well as your patients. Today's patient expects kind and considerate treatment in a medical office and asks for much more information about the course of medical care and various options.

The communication climate of a workplace does not stem from tasks employees are called on to perform. Instead, the communication climate results from how these employees feel about their tasks—and about each other. A positive communication climate can grow even in the most inhospitable physical surroundings, such as in an overcrowded and ill-equipped clinic, for example, if staff members have a strong sense of worth and mission. On the other hand, a well-appointed private practice could have a communication climate hampered by low morale. Whatever the setting, positive communication climates occur when employees feel valued, and negative climates occur when they feel unappreciated. Not so surprisingly, within a practice environment, there can be individual relationships that are either icy or warm, too.

Because morale is hard to quantify, business writers and management consultants tend to stick to topics that are easier to describe in numbers. In daily life, though, physicians and other leaders often find that their organizations work notably better if they adopt the attitude of consciously emphasizing improvement of the practice's communication climate. It is imperative that physicians remember that they are the leaders in creating the communication climate at their practice even as they build their staffs. Hiring practices can be made into morale-building techniques in use, too.

## Hiring and Morale Building

As Medical Group Management Association consultant Dick Hansen advises his physician clients, "Make it a priority to hire people who are friendly and kind—and evaluate staff performance in this area during reviews. Many management experts consider it literally impossible to train an employee to be nice when it's not in his or her nature," Hansen says. "Therefore, make sure that whoever does the hiring for your office recognizes the importance of 'the friendliness factor' when screening applicants. In addition, by adding a section on demeanor toward patients to staff evaluation, you let the staff know that friendliness, kindness, and respect for patients and staffers are considered key job responsibilities."

It is important to convey to job candidates during the interview process just how much the practice values qualities such as cordiality, handling of patients, and cooperativeness. The interviewing physician or staff member can give this information when he or she describes to the candidate what distinguishes the practice from the competition. If necessary, physicians and practice administrators can write up a script that lists the values to be underscored for use by interviewers.

Conveying the values of the practice during the job interview lets candidates know what kind of person and what qualifications will fit best with the needs of the practice. Some candidates may balk at the practice's expectations, but most candidates will find a practice's commitment to certain values to have a strong appeal. You are less likely to go wrong by discussing the practice's mission statement and values during the interview than by leaving such important information to the job candidate's imagination.

Morale and the resulting communication climate are important factors in keeping staff. After all, no one signs on for life. Physicians should take the lead in building staff morale. One simple, but often overlooked, way to bring some mood-lifting sunshine into your practice every day is to say a sincere "thank-you" to individual staff members whenever possible, Hansen emphasizes. He recalls one physicians' group with whom he consulted that "just couldn't bring themselves to thank the staff. They felt that these people worked for them, were paid to do their jobs, and shouldn't expect to be thanked." Such tough-mindedness about fine points may stem from the grueling training and demands placed on physicians themselves. In the face of such attitudes, a symbol of gratitude can sometimes substitute for verbal expression. In this case, Hansen finally convinced the physicians to buy doughnuts for the office once a week in appreciation of their staff's efforts.

## Don't Expect Staff to Pick Up Your Mess

Consultant Sally Jenkins believes that if you expect your employees to present a good face to your patients, it is up to you "to manage your emotions—no matter how you're feeling. After you've been in a tense situation . . . take a few seconds in the hall to consciously change your emotional mode. Then go in there and be friendly."

In other words, everyone in a fast-paced office has to make an attempt to distinguish among the various incidents and situations—good and bad—that are part of a normal workday. Often, it is hard to let go after delivering bad news or engaging in a tart exchange of words. We have to curb our natural tendency to carry past events into the present. Otherwise, there is a risk of a mess.

Sometimes, the mess is immediate and involves dragging someone into the turbulence of emotions that are not under control. After a difficult meeting, for example, a physician may take it out on a colleague who was not even in attendance. At other times, the mess means that someone has to follow along to clean up the aftermath of an outburst or inappropriate behavior. This is the case when a physician who is perturbed proceeds to upset a series of patients, who then must be calmed by staff members (a duty that the physician unconsciously expects these staff members to attend to).

In a departure from the more subservient mentality of the past, though, staff now will likely be less tolerant of the emotional mess that results from an abusive or disrespectful approach to their role. As Ken Hertz, administrator of the MacArthur Surgical Clinic in Alexandria, Louisiana, quips, "I used to be an arts administrator. So I like to say I've gone from prima donnas to 'prima doccas.'" Hertz does not hesitate to tell the ten surgeons in this multi-specialty group, "Screaming and yelling do not work. Don't throw charts because the nurse won't pick them up anymore."

According to Hertz, though, the physicians at MacArthur do show the necessary concern for the morale of the entire staff. Hertz points out daily examples: The MacArthur Clinic physicians personally paid for the uniforms of their entire staff, "one set for each day of the week," he notes. "Not only does this improve the overall look in the clinic, but there is something about seeing a reflection of yourself in your co-worker that engenders more teamwork."

"I encourage staff to talk directly to the doctor if they have a problem," Hertz continues. "He puts his pants on every day the same way you do," Hertz tells any of the 40 or so clinic staff members who come to him with their concerns or questions. "The docs are much happier this way, too," Hertz contends. "That kind of contact is good for staff and good for the doctors." Constant contact also means that staff members and physicians see one another as persons with a full range of motivations and abilities rather than occupants of niches in a hierarchy.

## Participation Raises Morale

In part, the positive communication culture found at the MacArthur Surgical Clinic can be attributed to Hertz's participative management style, which he advocates, "as opposed to just giving orders. I work from the bottom up and include staff a lot. For example, we recently purchased a new information system. The 'end-users' were involved in this decision from day one. They met with the vendors, had on-site visits, and they submitted something like RFPs (request for proposals) to the vendors."

Because the staff that will use this new billing/coding system must work together as a team, Hertz wanted them to make the initial purchasing decision as a team as well: "The doctor must communicate effectively to the nurse. The nurse must understand what the doctor has communicated, and the billing person must also understand."

His homespun talk notwithstanding, Hertz takes his role of staff spokesperson seriously. "I think of myself as their representative," he says. Because in his previous career he worked with classical musicians, Ken Hertz has placed an emphasis on bringing harmony to the communication culture at the MacArthur Surgical Clinic.

## Share the Perks

Perhaps most representative of the MacArthur Surgical Clinic surgeons' commitment to camaraderie is the annual employee holiday party, which is hosted each year by one of the surgeons at home. The clinic also sponsors a regular crawfish boil for staff and their families, and other popular outings (such as a baseball game) are scheduled for employees to share with family. Another social activity enjoyed by the entire clinic staff is their yearly Halloween costume competition. "We also decorate the clinic and sometimes include hospital staff in the fun. One year we invited the hospital's chief financial officer to judge our costume contest," recalls Hertz.

Special events like these celebrate the practice's accomplishments, underscore ties among colleagues, and express gratitude. As mentioned, showing appreciation helps to build morale. The playfulness of such events enables colleagues to communicate different aspects of themselves: You learn something about the self-perceptions of the ophthalmologist who appeared in a Superman costume at Halloween, the die-hard Yankees fan from billing who would not miss the baseball outing, and the nurses who dress to the nines for the holiday party.

A side benefit of social events is that a great deal of valuable information is exchanged in an informal setting. You may learn who is planning a wedding. You may also pick up such work-related information as who would like more challenge in their positions and who would like to add new skills by going back to school part-time.

## Communication as the Central Issue

Few issues have as much impact on our working lives as communication. The range of information needed to run an organization is considerable—from schedules and rates to diagnoses and prescriptions to telephone numbers and supply lists. Control of information gives an individual power, but the free flow of information within an organization actually leads to better morale, greater productivity, smoother management, and easier adaptation to change. While it is important to convey a practice's values to prospective staff members and current staff members, good internal communication will encourage all staff members, regardless of tenure, to adapt their behavior to the core qualities and mission of the practice, too. Physicians who adopt this approach may have to learn to manage with a light hand, but the rewards that they will receive are greater than the seeming loss of control.

### Bibliography

Murphy M. "Setting the right example." *Unique Opportunities.* Nov./Dec. 1998.

### Web Site of Interest

A large commercial site, www.work911.com, includes extensive book reviews. For a list of books that deal specifically with employee motivation, see www.work911.com/books/motivate/index.htm.

# Index

# Communication Tools to Help Build Your Practice

Effective communication plays a vital role in every medical practice—and building a successful practice requires the proper tools. With this in mind, the AMA offers a series of three targeted books to help physicians and practice managers improve communication skills with staff and patients.

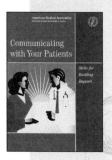

## Communicating with Your Patients: Skills for Building Rapport

Through real-life examples and sample dialogues, *Communicating with Your Patients* provides clear, proven strategies for communicating successfully with patients and their families, including information on how to:

- Break bad news
- Bridge culture gaps
- Work with difficult patients
- Develop trust with patients' families
- Interact with geriatric patients

Order #: OP208999BHS      Price: $34.95
ISBN#: 0-89970-973-1      AMA Member Price: $27.95

## Communicating with Your Staff: Skills for Increasing Cohesion and Teamwork

Offering practical information for use in any medical practice, this book helps physicians and practice managers to:

- Deliver helpful criticism
- Defuse and resolve conflict
- Maximize exchanges with staff of various ethnic groups
- Create a collaborative medical practice team
- Build a positive communication climate

Order #: OP208799BHS      Price: $32.95
ISBN#: 0-57947-000-9      AMA Member Price: $26.95

## Physician-Patient Relations: A Guide to Improving Satisfaction

This unique guide offers succinct advice on managing the challenges of physician-patient interactions, including how to:

- Assure patient retention and loyalty
- Identify obstacles to a good physician-patient relationship
- Assess patient satisfaction
- Build better communication skills

Order #: OP208699BHS      Price: $24.95
ISBN#: 0-89970-981-8      AMA Member Price: $19.95

**Phone orders: 800 621-8335**
**Secured online orders: www.ama-assn.org/catalog**

VISA, MasterCard, American Express and Optima accepted. State sales tax and shipping/handling charges apply. Satisfaction guaranteed or return within 30 days for full refund.

### Buy All 3 Books & SAVE 15%!

Price: $78.92      Order #: OP209400BHS
AMA Member Price: $63.62      ISBN#: 1-57947-187-0

American Medical Association
Physicians dedicated to the health of America

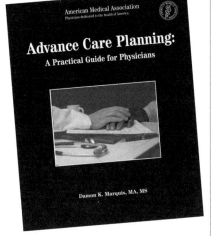